The State of the Internet: Living on the Network of Networks

Ryan Richardson Barrett

Published by Ryan Richardson Barrett, 2024.

THE STATE OF THE INTERNET: LIVING ON THE NETWORK OF NETWORKS

First edition. September 9, 2024.

Written by Ryan Richardson Barrett.

Book Cover Design by ebooklaunch.com

Also by Ryan Richardson Barrett

Watch for more at https://ryanrichardsonbarrett.com/.

Table of Contents

For my friend Zeppy, a cancer survivor.

Chapter 1 - Introduction

The thing nearly looks like clumps of fine string gathered together, forming sections separated by different brilliant shades of color. Many of the strands are grouped together and resemble small feather dusters, while in the center of the image exists a thick entanglement that crosses over all these brilliant colors. Altogether, the colorful strands make up a visualization of how the Internet is structured and how IP (Internet Protocol) addresses are organized together in order to communicate. A map of the Internet is as strange and beautiful as any geographic map.

Computer science is oddly intimate with psychology and, thus, sociology. This fact remains despite the presumed distance between biology (natural) and technology (synthetic). However, technology strives to improve human efficiency while humans strive to improve technology. Most systems of technology, such as AI (Artificial Intelligence) and computer programming languages, take direct inspiration from human activities and methodologies. Programming is human language translated into computer instruction, which is binary. Meanwhile, machine learning is a strategy for finding procedures or creating new methods of completing a task, which is both algorithmic and tangible in nature. Cybernetics is a field of study that handles turning complex decision-making into objectively explained processes. Society's thoughts and actions are more influenced by computer technology than ever, and another important relationship (perhaps the ultimate semantic relationship) grows more prevalent every day: the Internet.

To continue the theme of the close connection between computers and people, the Internet is effectively the world's largest conversation. The elaborate network that makes up the Internet is easily engageable by anyone with an Internet-connected device, and these devices have become prolific, resulting in the Internet of Things (IoT) and broader Internet access in nearly all countries. Some developing nations have mobile data Internet access that is better in quality than their drinking water.

The digital discussion carries on daily on ports 80 and 443. Internet access gives freedom to people who would otherwise live in a world that is thoroughly confined cognitively and even politically. No matter the limitations of someone's physical world, they can find freedom online with the right know-how. But, at the same time, the Internet can cause people immense issues with information overload and instill in them a reckless desire to constantly seek validation with unlikely satisfaction; Internet use can be addictive. Ultimately, the Web is as complicated as society, and subsequently, it is one of the best places to broadly evaluate humanity due to the mostly unregulated nature of the world online.

Humanity's collective conscious memories are available for anyone to sift through online. Fortunately, there are numerous technologies, one of which is search engines, to help climb the lofty mountain of madness online. There is no lack of stored information; in fact, there is potentially too much to sort through systematically. The ideas and data that are encapsulated by the Web are a substantial information explosion with waves that are still being felt by people today. The Web is far too elaborate to control, and most of the authoritarian control online is blatant censorship. People can make their own reasonable decisions about how they engage with the world's most expansive network, which is ultimately built by people, even if it is being more widely used by bots.

At some point, electronics become a network when they are connected to allow for communication. In this case, communication is the exchange of packets, the most simplistic form of data exchange. All of the CPUs (Central Processing Units), RAM (Random-Access Memory), capacitors, and other motherboard devices communicate together and make up a lone entity: a computer. But what is the required number of devices to form a network, and at what scale? Perhaps the entirety of the Earth is a network, seeing as how the open air contains enough radio frequencies from phone towers, satellites, and wireless access points to link humanity's collective conscience. Catching these frequencies that go dashing through the atmosphere between 2.4GHz and 6GHz, and coursing through copper cable veins that are strung along the Earth's surface, is easier than ever. No one is condemned to being trapped in a lonely world, yet everyone online is now doomed to hear the racket from the Web. Humanity is as connected and anxious as ever before. Yet, there is much hope in this bizarre network with which people have daily conversations. Some consciences carry too much guilt; others carry too little. The Internet seems to be cutting the deck to find a nice medium. A few things that were cut off, those being misinformation and bias, were only replaced by billion-dollar corporations peddling trash and turning ideologies into monetized products and services.

The Internet has completely changed...

Any number of words could be placed at the end of that sentence. *The State of the Internet* will explain several of the entities that have been drastically altered by the network of networks. Moreover, the ongoing development of the Internet as a whole is a true historical oddity, and that story will also be explained as well as gently expanded upon when looking at the future of the online world. In effect, the Internet connects ideas to a place where they are much more approachable to the common person.

Chapter 2 - History

B efore looking ahead, it is necessary to understand the unusual past of the Internet and how it developed into the modern Web. The World Wide Web is the main form of interacting with the broader Internet. The Internet, in its earliest form, was completely different than it is today. Finding websites or making connections to servers was usually accomplished by typing the domain name into a browser, which, of course, requires someone to know already where they want to go. When users had less specific knowledge about their end destination but understood the general type of site they were looking for, the search engine came into play and rapidly became a necessity when adventuring through the Web. Search engines are one of the key tools in using the Internet to its fullest extent, and they have progressed rampantly in the last three decades. Indexing the Web and being able to then search through those organized domains is how search engines have helped the Web develop.

Archie was the first ever search engine, and its name comes from the word "Archives." Barbados-born Alan Emtage developed Archie while studying and working at McGill University in Montreal in 1989, and the website was publicly launched in 1990. The archives that the engine sorted through were FTP (File Transfer Protocol) servers, which are simplistic servers that distribute files. In 1990, there was not much to find online. After searching with Archie, the site would return a list of related files that could be downloaded. FTP uses ports 20 and 21 for traffic, which helped Archie find these servers.

Several years passed before HTTP (Hypertext Transfer Protocol) and HTTPS (Hypertext Transfer Protocol Secure) websites were able to be searched for, which utilize ports 80 and 443, respectively.

Indexing the Web improved as developers realized how expansive the Internet was becoming and recognized the necessity of organizing it. Wandex (not to be confused with the modern search engine Yandex) was a bot created to scan and count websites in 1993 in an early effort to develop a headcount for the Web. The Wanderer was the script that perused through different websites to help measure the size of the Web at the time; Wandex was the actual index that the script produced. A user can only search for what they know, and so mapping out the unlinked ether that was the World Wide Web was quite the necessary undertaking in improving the Internet's usability, despite the fact The Wanderer was not a search engine, but it was a step towards developing such a thing. According to Wandex's creator Matthew Gray, "I was initially motivated primarily to discover new sites, as the Web was still a relatively small place."

• • • •

The element copper has been significantly important to human progress since its common use began in 4500 BCE, which signified the start of the Copper Age. Copper was used to make swords and knives, as it can be honed to an extremely fine edge. Coins were commonly made from copper because of their bright sheen and fairly consistent value. For thousands of years, copper has had diverse uses because of its unique attributes, such as being ductile and resistant to corrosion. In more recent centuries, telegraph lines used copper due to its conductive properties. Telegrams were one of the first forms of network communication, which only had a minuscule resemblance to what the Internet has become. Telegrams were the first time communication had been sent along a wire to locations across the globe. Copper lines are still vital to network communication today as both ethernet and coaxial cables primarily use copper to run a signal along the wire's length. At the peak of telegram advancement, the Telediagraph was engineered. Images could be sent over telegraph lines using the Telediagraph, and the Associated Press maintained a service called Wirephoto that enabled the Press to send photographs far faster than the mail was capable of.

Early Internet access was connected through phone lines and cable lines. More modern fiber optic lines are made from stretching clear glass or plastic that is then enclosed in layers of insulation. Fiber optic cables are then able to transmit flickers of light to transfer data. With the proper technology, Internet frequencies can be run on powerlines or any other electronically conductive wires, although broadband over powerline (BPL) has become more or less deprecated. BPL users would plug a modem into their wall socket to connect to the Internet that was being externally transmitted into their building's wiring.

Despite BPL being no longer popularly used, similar technology can transmit ethernet signals into a building's electrical wiring that originates from traditional fiber or cable Internet providers that are connected to a home or business. To explain further, an ISP (Internet Service Provider) sends ethernet to a typically wired building, and the modem translates it to an ethernet signal, which is then sent to a router, which is connected to an ethernet-to-wall socket adapter, which is then connected to a standard electrical wall socket. The ethernet-to-wall socket adapters are the key piece of technology; everything else is standard equipment for a home or small business's local area network. One adapter sends a signal from a router into the building's wiring while another adapter receives the data on the way out, which is then connected to a device via ethernet. The entirety of the building can utilize hardwired connections with this method, which would allow faster and more reliable connections than WI-FI if the building is quite large.

It is important to remember that homes and businesses are local area networks, which are subsequently part of wide area networks. Both entities then gather together to form the Internet. When a device connects to a website that is hosted across the world, networking hops are made to all kinds of obscure locations as packets are routed due to some locations not having simple direct routes to other places because the earth is full of many oceans and other geological barriers that cannot always be crossed with undersea lines or might lack satellite Internet coverage.

Before the creation of the Internet, computer networks were relegated to being only capable of communicating with a few other machines on a small network, such as what a university had at the time. Networks were not typically connected to other networks that were several miles away. The initial intent of ARPANET (Advanced Research Projects Agency Network) was to join these smaller networks together and was also supported by the United States Department of Defense for rapid communications. ARPANET began in 1969 and continued to proliferate throughout the United States as a network. Other types of networks existed at the time, but this period is generally referred to as being prior to X.25, a protocol for packet switching that would cause sweeping changes and marked an era shift. During the 1970s, various networks used different protocols, and different nations used varying protocols for packet-switching (the network exchange of data). Networks using differing protocols are roughly like people speaking different languages. Languages have meaning, but only to those who understand them. If networks were to communicate with one another, they needed to not only be connected but also configured to use the same protocol so data could be transferred and used by the sending and receiving parties. During this era, groups of computers slowly became a network of networks, which is one of the Internet's most astute names.

January 1st, 1983, was a very special day in history as it marked the Internet's birthday. This day marks the establishment of the commonly known protocol TCP/IP (Transmission Control Protocol/Internet Protocol), which was the first time computers had a universal means of sending and receiving packets. TCP was assigned port 1, beginning the allocation of early port assignments. However, it was not until 1989 that the Englishman Sir Timothy John Berners-Lee began work at CERN (Conseil Européen pour la Recherche Nucléaire) in Switzerland to create the World Wide Web, which subsequently became publicly accessible in 1993. Since then, websites have taken shape as pages written with hypertext markup language (HTML) that can be accessed by uniform resource locators (URLs). Berners-Lee leveraged a system of hypertext links to navigate from one page to another related page, allowing easier navigation online. The Internet is not exactly the same thing as the World Wide Web (which is what started the acronym WWW, known as "wuh wuh wuh" by Stephen Fry on his podcast Podgrams), even though the two terms are often used interchangeably. The Internet refers to the world's connected networks, while the Web refers to URLs or websites that are publicly accessible. If the Internet were a body, the Web would be its face.

CERN operates one of the longest-running websites, which began on August 6th, 1991. CERN completes research in physics and is home to the particle collider. Another antique website is the WWW VL (World Wide Web Virtual Library). The WWW VL is a huge compilation of links to websites curated by experts in their respective fields. The early 1990s saw the dawn of the Internet after its initial development in 1989. Most of the sites built during this time were owned and operated by universities and other research institutions, and they were acting participants in the upcoming age of online learning.

During this period, a metaphorical switch was flipped, and the Earth's most rapid form of communicating, connecting, and conversing awoke and has not gone to sleep since.

To move through a website, a user must go from page to page. Such an idea might seem strange, but consider the steps taken to navigate online. First, a person must open a web browser. Then, they might search for a phrase in the Omnibox (combined search bar and URL field nearly all browsers have) that is directly connected to a designated search engine. The search engine results page (SERP) Google and other search engines display contains links to sites, which subsequently also have links, and thus, the Web is navigated by traversing an intertwined yarn of pages that are all loosely connected. How many steps would it take to start on a news website like *The Verge* and end up looking at *Wikipedia*'s page for giraffes? Later, this (somewhat) critical information will be divulged.

The techniques for navigating the Internet only improved after Archie and Wandex were created, and networking became popular among other research centers, allowing them to share their pages on what was quite a small Internet of only about fifty different pages by the time 1993 came around. 1993 was a rapidly developmental year because CERN made their Web code royalty-free and released it to the public, resulting in more than a thousand websites being created that year. Of course, back-end code was very important in creating websites, but just as crucial in the progression of the Web was the introduction of a special web browser called Mosaic, an important player in how the front end of Web design changed. Mosaic was very modern for its time and allowed pages to be viewed with text and images on the same page when, prior to Mosaic, they would have to be viewed separately. Mosaic had a substantial influence on how websites were formatted and greatly contributed to a standardized (and more user-friendly) style of the webpage. The style Mosaic catered to looked kind of similar to a newspaper or magazine's layout, featuring headings, text, and images, although early websites contained numerous links to help in navigating the small but disorganized early Internet so users did not become digitally stranded. The popularity of

Mosaic caused Web developers to use a slightly more regulated format featuring images and words together, not just the two separated.

There are three eras in the Internet that describe the Internet in its entirety. Improvements in the broad Internet characterized each individual era of the online landscape. The era of Web 1.0 was very simple in terms of usability. The Internet was very small, and only professionals and members of academia used it. With more people using personal computers during the 1990s and corporations looking to capitalize on the dot-com bubble, Web 2.0 was brought into existence. Regular people wanted a Web they could easily engage with to do things like converse in chat rooms, read news which was now available instantly, watch videos, and complete research. The Web was the hot new place to be. Naturally, technology companies looked to capitalize on these human desires by creating websites where they quickly began to distribute advertisements. Today, companies like Meta and Google have become extremely proficient at serving ads to Internet users. Google, Meta, Microsoft, and other technology corporations significantly control the Web and what people see online, which is an important cornerstone of Web 2.0. Almost no privacy exists on the Web in today's age. Companies track what their website visitors do on their pages in order to serve them ads for products they are more likely to buy. Many companies also sell this information or share it with subsidiaries or anyone looking to buy, all in the name of targeting people with advertisements. However, now more than ever, anyone can create media online, sell products, and write articles, and thus, the concept of Web 3.0 is starting to come more clearly into view. Web 3.0 is intended to break up the old guard and decentralize the Internet. Web 1.0 and 2.0 were recognized after those eras had passed, Web 3.0 has not quite arrived, and the next generation will probably not develop in a clear and straightforward way. The Internet has many problems that need to be solved in terms of privacy and user experience before an entire new generation will form online.

Internet browsers have defined how being online feels. Individual sites have their own characteristics, but the way a browser is configured can make exploring online much more user-friendly, no matter the site. In 1994, the Navigator browser was created by Netscape, and it became the top dog in browsers, featuring integrations with Java and Javascript, allowing websites to be even more visually appealing and more interactive. In response to Navigator's introduction, Microsoft made their now famous (perhaps infamous) web browser Internet Explorer in 1995, which became standard on all Windows operating system installations, leading to much of its use. Internet Explorer likely led to the Web being more commonly referred to by its more encompassing name: the Internet. Gradual improvements occurred as the relationship between webpages and browsers worked in tandem to improve the Web. In 1997, cascading style sheets (CSS) were introduced, which served to make webpages much more appealing to view and, as a result, easier to maneuver through.

All of these progressions in the history of computer science led to a more humanistic phenomenon called the Information Age, which resulted in a modern information explosion. During the middle of the 1990s, the Internet became significantly easier for users to navigate, inspiring more people to become involved in using the Web to gain information as well as for entertainment. Prior to this period, using a personal computer had its purposes, such as for mathematical computations, writing documents, and other technical practices, but the desktop computer's interactions with networks definitely caused a flood of popularity during the dot-com bubble because people could suddenly buy things and find entertainment online.

The dot-com bubble was a time during the dawn of the Web when the stock market became overly saturated with companies that wanted an online presence and, in many cases, a storefront on the Web. Several companies seized this time to try and make their business more lucrative with the marketing help websites provided. However, many businesses did not see a substantial amount of practical improvements in their profits despite their rapid increase in popularity; shoehorning technology into companies does not automatically garner success. The type of advertising that the dot-com era gave to companies caused many public companies to see a huge surge in stock purchases. The considerable percentage of stock ownership caused stock prices to be greatly exaggerated amidst the high demand. Thus, a bubble formed, which was ready to pop by 2002 when investors realized their money was propping up less than successful companies.

Even today, stock valuation is a complex process that is only further complicated by wealthy and aggressive investors. Similar to the dot-com era, there are more recent trends in using the terms cloud and AI as keywords that business marketing teams now love to throw around. The technology sector seems especially vulnerable to bubbly stock prices that seem to soar as the result of non-tangible improvements in companies.

Chapter 3 – The Ever-Changing Internet

Since the Web's inception, rampant improvements have resulted in billions of people being interested in and actively accessing the Web. The number of devices that can access the Internet is increasing exponentially. Among the seemingly random list of devices on the Internet of Things are different types of thermostats accessed remotely, speaker systems, and even industrial machinery. The list goes on and on and certainly presents the question: Do all of these devices need to be connected to the Internet?

The Internet is running out of space, but not in a way that would be apparently obvious. There are only so many IP addresses that can be allocated to different devices. An IP address is a number that is designated to a device so routers are capable of finding the device on a network. That is what routers do; routers route packets eventually to devices people are using. Currently, IPv4 addresses look something like 192.168.1.1, which is a very common address assigned to a home or other building's router because that address ends in 1, making it the first IP on that subnet. Private IP addresses always begin with 192, 172, or 10 in the first octet. However, only a specific portion of those subnets can be used for private IP ranges. Public addresses can also begin with those three first octets, and the differences would begin in the second octet.

With a more technologically advanced group of devices communicating online (although many IoT devices have easily defeated security or simply none at all), more efficiency is required, and the protocols and ports used online have to keep up with the new increased traffic. Other changes in ports and protocols used online will affect firewalls and their capabilities to block bad traffic appropriately. As video and music streaming become commonplace online, these technologies are being refined to operate quicker, and IPv6 (Internet Protocol Version 6) will cause small improvements across the board in Internet usage. The incorporation of IPv6 into the mass of IPs the world uses is one of the most impactful changes the Internet has ever gone through. IPv6 addresses are more easily transferred than IPv4 (Internet Protocol Version 4), and IP addresses are at the core of any network and, therefore, the Internet.

IPv4 addresses require Network Address Translation (NAT) to have packets navigate to where they need to go. IPv6 does not require this type of mapping because its IPs are unique and are never translated. This is a case of intuition over brute-force computational power. On most networks, Dynamic Host Configuration Protocol (DHCP) is used to automatically assign IPs to new devices on the network. IPv6 has a built-in feature to something similar itself, although not all routers support IPv6 doing this.

Considering how there are only 4,294,967,296 IPv4 addresses (for simplicity's sake, the private IPs in that scope can be ignored), the public Internet will run out of addresses to use in the IPv4 format. Compared to ten years ago, there are substantially more devices that need their own unique IP, and although IPs are recycled, two cannot be active at once. So, the obvious solution to this conundrum is there needs to be a different type of IP address, and thus the new scheme

IPv6 was created. The IPv6 structure of IP addresses contains 2^{128} unique IPs, which is such a staggering number it should suffice for the foreseeable future. Outside of better network function, IPv6s simply fulfill the task of needing more IPs. An example of an IPv6 address is 2001:0000:130F:0000:0000:09C0:876A:130B, which uses both numbers and letters to create addresses and has four spots per subnet rather than three. Currently, IPv4 addresses are the most common, and it will take an unspecified number of years before IPv6 addresses become the most popular IP used online. Globally, IPv6s make up roughly 40% of IPs in use, while in the US, that number is closer to 50%, and the new IP standard becomes more prevalent every year. IPv6s have simpler routing and can more directly make hops from start to finish as packets navigate to their destination. Simpler packet headers are another reason for the more efficient transfer of the packet and a reduction in unimportant header fields. In 2009, Verizon made the move to require devices connecting to its mobile LTE (Long Term Evolution) network to use IPv6 addresses as the new standard. The plethora of smartphones out and about is exploding in developing countries, while they have been commonplace for nearly two decades in more wealthy nations. Smartphones certainly require the use of IPv6 because smartphones are the most common way for users to access the Internet, and the huge mass of these devices requires an equally huge amount of IP addresses to accommodate them. Worldwide, nearly seven billion smartphones are in use.

• • • •

The technology company Starlink is worth discussing due to its unique approach to satellite networking to provide customers with Internet access. Under the right conditions at night, Starlink satellites are frequently visible in places where they commonly orbit. Starlink, a satellite Internet technology, is unique in how it handles networking. Other types of satellite Internet are common enough, but those satellites orbit farther from Earth and function differently than Starlink. Antennae are positioned by the person using the service on the ground, which then connects directly to the Starlink low-orbit satellites. Starlink can potentially avoid several of the hops it would otherwise take to route Internet packets to their final destination. However, there would need to be quite a few satellites, and they would need to be located in the proper position for the purported speed compared to fiber optic lines and copper, but Starlink does bring about a new approach to routing packets to different intermediary locations with potentially lower latency because of the fewer hops the connections must make. This company certainly will not be the last to utilize this creative method of using a low-orbit satellite network.

Phones and tablets have become prolific users of the Web, and Android and iOS phones have altered the structure of networks because of how they connect to phone towers, which can broadcast up to nearly forty-five miles away. These towers broadcast their signal to form large networks of smartphones and other devices that use mobile data. Rapidly, more of the world is being covered in mobile network access, which glues network users together while they toss around packets as they complete tasks online. In geographically smaller nations like

Costa Rica and Trinidad and Tobago, their populations have 100% mobile data coverage, while larger nations like the US and Canada have 99.9% and 99% coverage, respectively, according to the International Telecommunication Union. The fact that radio waves have gone from being used for the earliest radio broadcasts in 1920 in Pittsburgh to covering much of the world with Internet access is clear evidence of how far this technology has come in just over one hundred years.

The Internet and the usability of technology have changed massively since 1983. One of the most aggressively overtaken, assaulted, and rapidly destroyed industries that have been led nearly to ruin by computers and the Internet is the clock industry. Any smartphone user (even if they are only an occasional user) has had the lowly alarm clock removed from their life like an ex-spouse moving to Greenland. Many public places no longer have clocks hanging on their walls because there is little reason, considering most people carry a phone or even a smartwatch with them. People in the early 1990s probably had no idea their ticking jewelry and old grandfather clocks would be deemed obsolete so quickly. Humans who leverage technology in their daily lives are becoming more ingrained in the collective networks of the online community, which is ultimately made by people. Smartphones are humanity's primary means of connecting their lives to a computer and, furthermore, the Internet. Frequently, people start their day by turning off an alarm on their phone and then mindlessly sorting through notifications.

Due to the very brief delays in network communication from one side of the Earth to another, it was inevitable that the Internet would overtake several traditional services. The first example of this was fax machines acting more rapidly than traditional mail. Obviously, physical mailboxes are still full of letters (many of which no one wants), but faxing was definitely easier and perhaps simpler than writing a letter and putting it out to be mailed. However, fax machines technically used phone lines and modems and were not assigned IP addresses, so they were not the same sort of networking device as computers and other Internet-connected devices. The Internet has permitted significantly faster communications and embodies the term instant gratification.

In the 1960s, messages could be sent between computers on connected networks, but it was not until 1983 that ARPANET began using a critically important technology: email. In 1983, the SMTP (Simple Mail Transfer Protocol) protocol was born, and humanity grew even more rapidly sociable with their written conversations. People could now converse via text with a delay in sending and receiving of mere seconds. IMAP (Internet Message Access Protocol) and POP (Post Office Protocol) are two other popular protocols for email servers, both of which have improved since their inception over three decades ago.

Despite substantial improvements in electronic mail, including applications, message size limits, and email application improvements, email has been the staple Internet communication method and is visually similar to its original design. Much has changed in the online world, but email is so robust and simple that it has remained a constant over the years. Due to cloud storage, sharing large quantities of files is easier than ever using systems like Google Drive. The standard maximum for email size is 10MB. Nearly all operating systems come with an email application by default packaged with their system, while using a web browser is, of course, another popular way to log in to a person's email account. The dawn of email was the first time people were given what is more or less a username, a Web persona outside of their own name. Email addresses are now integral to people's identities, and typically, creating an inbox is the first thing a new Internet user would do the first time they visit the Web. Making an account on any online platform nearly always requires an email address, so it has become a modern necessity. Every day, people's personage becomes more ingrained in the world online with social networking sites, but the start of all of this was the name personage they assigned to their inbox.

The Internet has replaced many services. Online banking has greatly streamlined the otherwise joyous experience of standing in line at a bank to move money from a checking to a savings account or vice versa. Relationships between individuals have changed as a result of voice and video communication improving vastly in the last ten years. Now, it is easier than ever to message someone, speak to them, or have a video call. Applications like FaceTime, WhatsApp, Zoom, Skype, and Discord all have the capability of engaging two or more people in a video call. The technical advancements in the backbone of the Internet have been vital to its success, but the more humanistic side of the Web is how it is changing people.

Society does not have much further to go in recreating a physical in-person meeting. The most advanced technology in this realm lies in VR and MR (Virtual Reality and Mixed Reality), which uses headsets and hand controllers to digitize an experience that closely resembles what it would be like to be with someone in person. Later on, systems like the Valve Index and the Meta Quest Pro will be discussed in the chapter "An Adventure on the Internet," as these devices are bringing a classic in-person conversation into the digital world.

Discussing the Internet is not dissimilar to discussing the weather because they both can change in a brief amount of time. The ebb and flow of the online community and global discussion that takes place on the Web alter what people require for their various wants. The raucous and extremely rapid success of social media has turned humanity's eye to this technology as a total change in culture and society, and this phenomenon is only one of the first of many. Humanity's mirror may turn a new face in a matter of months as fast as information can be exchanged online these days. Trends are exhausting. Today, good ideas gain momentum from all the voices of the world, and they are being listened to in a new way. Technology as a whole gains life from its own momentum, and it is difficult to conceive what appealing new concepts will thrive online in just a matter of months. Finding things online has never been easier.

Chapter 4 – Searching the Web

Today, navigating the Web is easier, yet more treacherous than ever.

Strangely enough, a modern and forward thinker named Vannevar Bush conceptualized search engines in 1945 in his essay "As We May Think." An excerpt from Bush's essay states: "Science has provided the swiftest communication between individuals; it has provided a record of ideas and has enabled man to manipulate and to make extracts from that record so that knowledge evolves and endures throughout the life of a race rather than that of an individual." Most of the technology that Bush was around during his time was mechanical in nature, and electronics were quite simple; in fact, vacuum tube systems (similar to hydraulics) were some of the most advanced electrical systems he would have engaged with. Bush was concerned by the lack of organization in scientific papers and desired a more straightforward way to access documents for research purposes; Bush wanted an easily accessible catalog for scientific papers. Bush managed this task despite the fact there was significantly less to be searched than there is now –not much to do online either, considering the Web's birth was four decades away. Vannevar Bush certainly had incredible foresight. Furthermore, he also had some early ideas about linking documents together in a tangible way, which was one of the earliest published concepts similar to what hyperlinks would become, and hyperlinks are critical to how search engines function.

Indexing is necessary for search engine functions. Search engines are crucial for mapping the Internet. Google has become a significant juggernaut in the search engine world. An estimated 90% of search engine use belongs to Google as far as the number of queries goes. Due to how most webpages are organized via subheadings, text, and links, Google crawls these coded attributes to find search results. Because of this structure, many website developers are following specific designs to best accommodate Google, which is called SEO (Search Engine Optimization). For Google to recognize what is possible to produce as a result, it must have a figurative map of where things are, which is achieved by leveraging crawlers that search out sites and download assets from the Web. Assets are then regurgitated, such as in Google Images search results. However, before Google can reproduce media, it must be indexed, meaning it must be mapped to a location. As a side note, a key difference between the Clearnet and the dark web is the fact that search engines cannot index locations on the dark web or present assets from that part of the Internet. All of Google's indexed locations are stored in a massive database that recalls the locations when search terms are entered. Indexing also involves algorithms determining what a webpage is about so it can better understand how to serve content that matches search criteria.

Google is one of the largest and most well-known technology companies operating today. Much of Google's success began with its search engine, which became publicly available in 1998 but was previously used on Stanford's private college network before then. Later on, Google grew into a much larger company and became publicly traded in 2004.

More people think of Google as a search engine than a complete and broad tech company, but Google and their subsidiaries, Google Brain and DeepMind, have made groundbreaking impacts in artificial intelligence platforms such as Gemini, one of the first multimodal AI platforms. Multimodal AI systems can interact with data from text, video, and sounds, unlike more traditional chatbots, which focus solely on language modeling.

Searching the Web has become a critical part of developing AI systems. AI greatly relies on data, and without *Wikipedia* and other text corpora, language models would not be able to be developed because they require a tremendous amount of text to improve their text-generation capabilities and the digital knowledge these platforms can recall. The way these large text bodies are used frequently does not involve their original creator's permission, which can be copyright infringement.

Yahoo! Search began in January of 1994 and soon after became the Web's most popular engine of search. Two years later, in 1996, Robin Li patented a system to rank webpage search results called RankDex, and this system helped improve search engine results. Li went on to found Baidu, a Chinese search engine.

Ranking is a very important aspect of how search engines show their users (hopefully) relevant results. RankBrain has become a vital technology for Google's search engine. RankBrain is an AI algorithm that is trained on people's Google searches. The main principle of RankBrain is to show a searcher content that best fits what they want to find. Search engine optimization strategies can manipulate search engines into displaying content from sites that are highly optimized, even if their content is not entirely relevant or even what the person searching wants to find. Neural matching is another strategy that Google uses to better understand what a search query means, but it also recognizes what a website page contains so that these two factors can be determined to be similar. Google is not overly specific about what mechanisms they use in their search engine, and open source engines, in general, are not commonly used to search the Web. Engines like Swirl, Apache Solr, and Elasticsearch are open-source projects, but they are mostly used at the enterprise level to sort through databases. Typically, the databases could contain formatted data that pertains to sales that are organized by columns such as date and value of a sale. Additionally, networking logs can be searched with this type of search engine, and logins and account manipulations can be shown. Open-source search engines are used to organize large amounts of data quickly.

Bert (Bidirectional Encoder Representations from Transformers) was developed into the AI system Gemini, but Bert's name is an important reference to how the language model functions and, furthermore, how search queries are understood by the engine. When people read sentences in English and many other languages, they grow to understand what they mean by reading the sentences from left to right. More traditional LLMs (Large Language Models) do not read; they simply analyze each word individually in the sentence, which does not always work well because, obviously, the order of words in a sentence is critical to understanding its meaning. LLMs do not really use context like a person would, although models are rapidly improving. Bert's bidirectional aspect is very important because it allows the LLM to analyze a search phrase forward and backward from any given word in the phrase, making it more advanced than other language models. This type of analysis helps the model recognize patterns and similarities to different Googled phrases. Understanding the intent of a searcher is important in helping search engines know what they are trying to find. An advanced system like Gemini also analyzes the pages it is considering for display. If a person were to google "How much butter do you put into chocolate chip cookies?" algorithms would need to find cookie recipes and not commercially made cookies' contents, as those would complicate the results and potentially return an unhelpful response. In May of 2024, Google launched its new AI Overviews search results feature. Although the feature does a good job of combining responses, some of the responses are wildly inaccurate. This search system is currently in a testing phase, and Google has taken action to remove many of the incorrect and incoherent responses.

Word proximity, or the relevance individual words have in the context of a phrase based on their location, was an important process to iron out as search engines became more advanced. People prefer not to have to write code when they search, so recognizing nuances of written language is very important when searching algorithms are built. Search engine creators encourage websites and searchers alike to use terminology in a normal way when building their sites and creating a search query. The reason for this is to accommodate search engines and to help them find features on webpages that are indeed what people are looking for. The alternative to this is to follow strict SEO strategies that often create mundane and useless websites full of keywords and repetitive formatting that do not help a person. Many of these sites exist to sell a product or service. Machine learning needs to better understand human language, as opposed to people having to craft searches to find what they are looking for. Naturally, that goal is not always achieved, but understanding search habits and website structure has helped search engines improve. Google and Bing intend for their platforms to be as user-friendly as possible. As AI algorithms improve to better understand written language, results will improve accordingly. Training data is critical to how Google and Bing function, and it is difficult to maintain a system of input (search query) and output (Search Engine Results Page) for all possible results, especially considering how people usually search for new and possibly obscure things on the Internet.

• • • •

Shopping for things on the Web is really fun. With the help of a piece of plastic with numbers on it and, as always, an Internet connection, people can buy just about whatever they want online. From couches to cobras, most things can be purchased from the Web, and the dot-com bubble did have at least one lasting impact, which is that most businesses maintain an online presence so customers can at least find them, if not also be able to order products from them directly.

The Internet has some unusual effects on the cost of living and the economy as a whole. Practically all major businesses have a website, which has brought a significant amount of competition to the global marketplace. Businesses without much of an online presence still sell their goods on Amazon, Wal-Mart, and other mass retailers. In the past, people had to rely on local businesses for goods. In more rural communities, these storefronts did not always have what consumers were looking for, and the scarcity of various goods in a region caused prices to be higher. The Internet has promoted a new level of competition in business, and companies have had to accommodate different pricing schemes, whether lower or higher.

Clothing and shoes make up close to three-quarters of the items purchased online by people in the US. The stylistic taste of people is difficult to satisfy, and an article of clothing like socks or t-shirts is extremely easy to mail in a small package that is not likely to be damaged when it is shipped. According to *Forbes*, e-commerce sales in 2024 are expected to grow by 8.8% since 2023. Of course, because of the increased demand for online goods, shipping companies have also had to substantially increase their workload in the last decade.

Nowadays, the Internet has made it easier for consumers to find good businesses and businesses to find good consumers. Nearly all successful businesses, such as Walmart and Target, operate in a brick-and-mortar storefront as well as an online store. Regional limitations have also been nullified by modern businesses' ability to cheaply mail packages to their shoppers. Even food is becoming more readily available to be purchased online, and non-perishables bought in bulk can be sold from a digital storefront that rarely has rivals in physical shops. In terms of more immediate and hot meals, delivery services like DoorDash and Grubhub success were spurred on by travel restrictions during the COVID-19 outbreak.

First comes communication, and then comes action. In this case, communication is the Web, and the action is logistics. Stores online rely on mail, trucking, sea freight, and other transportation methods to get their products to buyers rapidly and undamaged. Today, it is easier than ever to buy a product from another continent and receive the item in less than a week, whereas local items can be delivered within hours in some cases.

Clothing and food are not the only necessities people look to the Web for. Purchasing items related to travel and tourism, such as plane tickets, cruise tickets, and hotel rooms, is made considerably easier. Evaluating prices between flights would be fairly miserable without various comparison sites online.

Currently, on Amazon, some of the best-selling and highest-rated items are gummies, energy drinks, plenty of chips, bars, nuts, and spices. Anyone online (and hungry) could easily assemble an excellent meal from foods and spices bought and mailed to their house, and again, this has increased competition and availability for consumers.

Not everything is perfect on the Web when it comes to buying and selling; there can be significant conflicts between parties, sometimes to the point of legal action. The integrity of many businesses has been brought to light through online reviews that have spoken on how well different businesses and organizations serve the public. This accountability has greatly helped relations between communities and businesses, which can often be at odds. In the cases where businesses are not operating in a way that customers can enjoy, shoppers and patrons can speak up online about the establishment's shortcomings. Extremely popular websites such as Yelp,

Angie's List, Google Business Profile (which also contains information like a store's address and hours), and Facebook all contribute to building a Web platform to converse about businesses. If a hungry individual looking for restaurants online wants to find an image of a restaurant's menu, they probably can.

The BBB (Better Business Bureau) also operates in the US and Canada to improve consumer/business relations. As the BBB puts it: "The BBB helps people find businesses they can trust." The BBB's website allows people to search for businesses and see the complaints that people have left, and the BBB also shows if a business is accredited with them. Other review platforms are significantly less formal than the BBB because this 'Bureau' is a nonprofit that acts as a go-between in protecting consumers from bad business practices.

Later, more humanistic and intangible searches will be discussed.

Chapter 5 – Faltering Search Engines

One strange feature of the Internet is how it brings about a collective consciousness among people. Because many of the thoughts and ideas of people are now on the Internet, this consciousness is quickly becoming shared. As people witness different popular ideas (some of which are more accurately described as mob mentalities), the Internet can be a substantially irritating and uncomfortable place at times, especially on social media sites. The amount of information that is available online is overwhelming, and the shock factor of disturbing content is becoming more exaggerated as clickbait has become a mainstay of numerous forms of media. Witnessing violence and other traumatic events that are readily displayed by social media has become commonplace as the shock factor of thumbnails and article titles attract clicks. Advertisements are even more vehement than videos and articles. They play up strange images to draw people's attention as they browse, and some sites contain dozens of ads that rudely deluge their visitors so they can advertise their wares.

Image and video content on the Internet is making rare events seem more common. One example of this is how easy it is to find videos of storms, many of which were recorded in the last decade. Videos of weather rarities like tornadoes are now easy to find on the Weather Channel's website and other video sites, despite the fact these storms are difficult and often dangerous to film, which initially prevented their filming. IoT devices with cameras, such as smart home cameras and vehicle dashcams, in the past, would have been very difficult to prove that there was a tornado other than by a meteorologist evaluating an area that had been struck by a suspected tornado and surveying the damage the high winds had caused. Now, the likelihood that someone has filmed one of these storms is much more common, and there are thousands of amateur recordings of unusual storms that make their home on the Internet. People enjoy engaging with rarities, and that phenomenon has altered what those same people believe to be common occurrences.

The standard of knowledge and the quality of its indexing are changing, and search engines are making that possible and enhancing the effects of that change. Anyone can learn anything by using the Web, and search engines frequently curate that information. Knowledge can be very overwhelming, and when all of humanity's collected information is readily accessible, it is not difficult to become completely distraught by this absolute flood of information. However, confirmation bias can result from using search engines in an inappropriate way. A user may search for a phrase like, "Is broccoli bad for you?" This immediately searches all the possibilities of how to be harmed by broccoli, despite the fact broccoli is a vegetable that has numerous nutrients such as sulforaphane, which can hinder and stop cancer growth. Broccoli is not a harmful vegetable, and reasonable consumption of broccoli has health benefits. When specific words appear in a query the search engine is intended to search, bias is immediately instantiated into this quest for information. Syntax and word choice are the most important aspects of searching, as the individual words in a string are the easiest to analyze, as opposed to the collective string. The phrasing of searches is also important to what the results will be, but human phrasing can be difficult to analyze. Because of the human connections that exist via the Internet, when a user finds information made by another person catering to what was searched for, these irrational assumptions can be affirmed. Search engine optimization can also lure people into venturing to their site, which may be barely even adjacent to what a person is looking for and often contains inaccurate information that bolsters their products or improves their business interests. Unfortunately, the Web is perfect for catering to social bubbles that breed bias and collectivize degeneracy. If a researcher wants to make something true, the Internet contains enough nonsense to falsely convince the researcher of their falsehood.

Denizens of the Web do not just bring their bias to search engines; search engines themselves show censored and altered information. Many questions that people search might be phrased to perfectly match a solution that exists out there in the ether. Subtle differences in phrasing can completely change the results of a search. One of the most immediate conflicting issues in search engines is advertisements being embedded into the results. Companies paying to have their products and services placed higher on page results can sway a user into thinking that certain products are more popular than they really are. Websites like Amazon and other online stores use this method of advertisement on their own sites' search bar. Since searching the Web has become an important stream of information for millions of people around the world, it is necessary that engines provide information with as much accuracy as possible. However, most engines use metadata and cookies to track what a searcher regularly looks for. Differentiated user profiles can provide custom results for a searcher, which could possibly benefit them at the expense of accuracy. Search engines note a searcher's geographic location to serve them results like local restaurants when searching for good places to eat.

In terms of more technical searches, having multiple sources is as important as ever, but that is not easy to do when certain engines proliferate and accidentally spread incorrect answers. Misinformation begets misinformation, and the mob mentality is alive and well on the World Wide Web. Once someone learns a piece of inaccurate information, they may never let go of that fallacy.

Neither Google nor Bing is able to clearly explain how their search engines function and much of that is due to the dynamically changing nature of the Web and the engines themselves. AI models embedded in search engines might handle obscure searches in unknown ways. Furthermore, the proprietary technology involved with search algorithms is not something companies want to give away for free. Search engine optimization has become a buzzword that describes how things like websites can be crafted to be most easily found by search engines, usually to sell things and increase a company's online visibility. SEO researchers are some of the most knowledgeable people regarding how search engines function, but they are not affiliated with an actual company that manages an engine. In a similar vein of technology, hackers can sometimes know more about a program than its developers. Tech companies have been racing to develop the leading search engine for close to three decades.

SEO is partially to blame for why search results are becoming more crowded with the same things even though they are not explicitly relevant to what was searched. SEO focuses on how a website is configured while considering things like keywords, content quality, metadata, and crawlability, which all allow engines to acquire more data from the site. If a search engine is able to easily index a website, that website is going to appear frequently in search results. Frequently, the heavy-handed nature of SEO can make websites appear to be a slurry of ill-suited buzzwords. Many websites contain fairly useless blogs, such as a page of the site that is an article laden with keywords that improve search ranking. Another way sites instantiate SEO is by having a Q&A section that closely matches the questions someone types into Google, Bing, Duck Duck Go, or their favorite search engine. Things like subheadings and the overall organization of a website can improve its ranking online while incidentally making it look worse in the eyes of a person. In general, most people agree that SEO works well for businesses and badly for humans seeking honest information or products. The conflicting parties, those being tech companies and SEOs, are working in tandem to incidentally worsen the content on the Internet and make it less relevant and more commercialized. Much of this has made the Internet a more hectic place to navigate, whereas the purpose of the Internet (and any computer network) is to improve and better organize communication. Fortunately, many journalists have exposed tech companies for showing biased results as well as inaccurate information on their SERP, which was often due to AI being stuffed into scenarios where it is not apparently practical. Google claims that websites that best suit people are most likely to appear as search results and that SEO is not supposed to be able to manipulate their algorithms. None of this seems to be true because many SEO techniques are used prolifically to improve the site's SERP ranking.

Google uses a metric called E-E-A-T (Experience, Expertise, Authoritativeness, and Trustworthiness) in their search engine, but E-E-A-T is used in a way that is fairly unknown outside of Google. E-E-A-T was created to help Web developers create sites that contain accurate information that will then be favored by Google. SEO-minded people are also very attentive to these four characteristics in terms of properly manipulating their websites to meet these standards. Somewhat confusingly, according to Google, these attributes do not reflect how search results are ranked, i.e., how high a certain result appears in the list. There is further controversy as to whether Google uses data from the same user's Chrome to customize search results. Locational searches, like the aforementioned restaurants or local businesses someone is searching, may have a pertinent bias, but censorship by way of the complete removal of websites is embarrassing for an American company or any anti-authoritarian institution to implement in their technology. Removing the searcher's opportunity to disdain the removed content is an assumption of control by corporations, and there is no practical purpose in censoring an entity that shares information. Open communication is clearly what the Internet is intended for.

The most important part of how a website recognizes and maintains information on a user is with cookies. Anyone who has ever visited a website has probably been asked by the site if they could give permission to store cookies on their device. Even if not prompted, many sites still store some form of data.

A web browser stores the cookies locally and gives these metadata files to the site when connecting. The reason an account is still logged in when returning to a site is because of authentication cookies. Other cookies monitor what is clicked on a website, such as an online store continuing to show visitors items they have viewed previously. In countries a part of the European Union, it is law to state a website uses cookies for nonessential purposes. Google has stated they use cookies to store user preferences, but it is not well known what other uses these cookies are for, and this varies by website.

· · · ·

In 2010, Microsoft and their subsidiary, Foundem, were concerned about Google's ability to make themselves less present in Google, and this challenge of compromising anti-trust laws went to court. During the proceedings, it was ruled that Google took actions to improve its customer experience and was not doing anything wrong by removing content from competing companies.

A similar bias is imposed against services that Google competes with, such as Google Maps. The company MapQuest is usually not shown as high-ranking a search result as Maps, but that could also be because more people use Google Maps. Monopolization on the Internet is not uncommon, but preventing these companies from being successful is not always coherent or appropriate, although a search engine selling products it bolsters is concerning.

Establishing how a search engine should operate and be regulated is difficult because demanding that Google show how its search engine works would be giving away secrets of a highly lucrative technology. Not being clear-cut makes it easier to accuse search engine companies of being biased because it is difficult to prove they are not, as Google hoovers up more market share every day in the realm of search engines. Fortunately, there will always be competitors for Google and Bing, and many of these engines work well for specific purposes, such as viewing pages the big two intentionally remove from the results page. Some of the best software available is open-source because that means thousands of people have scoured over the source code, have a good grasp of how it works, and can recognize if it functions appropriately. The closed systems Google and Bing maintain will always be difficult to understand, and thus, speculation is only increasing about how these search engines function.

Since the dawn of search engines, just before the mid-nineties, search engine optimizers have tried (and often succeeded) to game the system. In time, search engines have always responded by trying to nullify these strategies. One of the earliest and most successful manipulations of search engines was creating a litany of pages that link to the website that is being bolstered. This large group of pages makes the target site seem more popular in the figurative eyes of engines. Because of how search engines index pages, having lots of links to a page online will make it more popular in search results. Google, Microsoft, and Yahoo are not the only parties responsible for making the Web worse by turning search results into a cesspool of corporate jargon. How often have you queried a search engine with a question for it to supply information that clearly had a narrative to solve your problem with a product the website was selling? These businesses are hiring professionals to better commercialize solutions. After all, the main purpose of a business is to provide a solution, and unfortunately, search engines are looking for honest, direct information when they end up becoming entangled by indexing that leads to SEO-heavy pages. Business bias often does not provide the best solution when they are permitted to alter their visibility online. The back-and-forth rhetoric between search engine developers and businesses will continue. Search engine developers accuse SEOs of taking advantage of their systems, while SEOs generally have the opinion that search engines are simply too easy to take advantage of. What other type of online advertisement is better than getting Google or Bing to showcase a company's website? Digital libraries and Web resources like Britannica and *Wikipedia* help to provide free, unbiased information that is more accurate (and better cited) than many alternatives. While it is easier than ever to find information online, the accuracy of that information may be growing more questionable.

Chapter 6 – Unique Methods of Searching

Despite the fact that search engines have become more biased and easily manipulated by businesses and other organizations that take formulaic steps to enhance their Web visibility, search engines have also developed into the leading way to find and research things online. With adequate skills and a little bit of creativity, finding obscure things on the Web has become easier than ever, although search engines are not the only avenue for discovering things.

Google has implemented a feature they refer to as AI Overview, which uses the model known as Gemini to give a collective search result. The essence of what Gemini is doing is sorting through sites on the Web and producing an answer that is an amalgamation of what it finds. To surmise from earlier, many of these results are helpful from a distance, but other times, they can be inaccurate because their sources are untrue or poorly written. Gemini itself may also have flaws that cause it to produce wildly inaccurate results. Although an elaborate overview can help with some more drawn-out questions, which are algorithmically analyzed as specific parameters, doing so can lead to oversights in accuracy. An example of this would be searching for "green corduroy pants near me that cost less than $100 and are highly rated." Unfortunately, finding information online is a piece of cake, while finding accurate information online is much more complex. Web users have numerous search tools at their disposal, which is fortunate because the Web is not easy to navigate. Summarizing multiple sources into one frequently works better for a person than relying on one entity's ideas, whether that be a random forum-style post or a vetted Web article such as from a university. AI models attempt to use a similar strategy, but their lack of cognition can cause these models to falter.

People can be extremely intelligent, but their memories struggle to be as broad and easy to recall as AI model's datasets are. AI platforms, through search engines, are becoming more conversationally proficient (at least on the listening side of the conversation) and are slowly becoming increasingly capable of accepting more elaborate queries that require multiple answers rather than one simple response. Search engines improving at organizing text and comprehending specific features of language (like slang used in queries) will help people find what they are looking for on the Web.

• • • •

Although text-based searching is the most popular method of searching the Web, there are several other technologies that can be used to great effect. One such form of searching that both Google and Bing are capable of completing is reverse image searches. Reverse image searches involve someone uploading an image or giving an image's link to the engine, which then attempts to find images that closely resemble the initial image that was being searched for. AI computer vision (CV) models have greatly helped in improving how this technology works. Computer vision evaluates images for things like edge lines, colors, and image size to determine what images are similar by discerning what they contain. Some images are indeed best described by an image; typing out exactly what is being searched for is not always the easiest way to find a picture. Machine learning algorithms do well when assigning characteristics (features) to an image, and these variables are not described by language. For example, edge lines usually show the rough perimeter of an image, such as the outline of a person's face. A face is difficult to perfectly describe to a search engine when making a query. However, as all the major search engines improve their systems of search, search queries are able to more closely resemble human language because that will cater to most people, and an important goal of the philosophy of AI is that the technology should be able to communicate well with text and other forms of human communication. That fact was understood as far back as Turing's time of research in the 1950s.

A drawback of text-based searches is that those kinds of searches are best at finding other related text, which is the simplest explanation for how the algorithm functions. Anyone who has searched for a song but could not remember any lyrics can relate to the drawbacks of text-based searching. For several years, there have been applications for Android and iOS that will sample a song being played aloud by using its speaker and then find what that song is via soundwave comparison. Similar extensions exist for web browsers, which enable a user to find out what a song is while the application listens to a movie or video that is being played in the browser. With companies like Google DeepMind working to incorporate practical (as opposed to cumbersome and useless) AI applications into their search engine, more types of media may be able to be searched, such as documents and other files. Written language is rather limiting when it comes to exploring the scope of the Internet, and theoretically, using search criteria consisting of a sound or image file could yield better results if Google continues to improve its machine learning algorithms in its engine.

For now, Google and Bing have numerous features that are not too commonly known. Google has an Advanced Search feature that can be accessed by clicking Advanced Search near where the search query is entered on their homepage. Advanced Search allows a user to restrict the results to a certain time period as well. When looking for information online, such as something time-sensitive like the stock market, searching for webpages that were created recently may be pivotal. Furthermore, finding a past event that was known to be relevant during a certain timeframe can also be easily searched for. There is also a Tools tab located below the search bar that displays a few of the more Advanced Search features without having to navigate away from the previously input query.

Please note that search terms are put inside of quotations to visually separate the search query in the following paragraphs. Quotes are not intended to be used literally, as that would have an adverse effect on the search because they will be treated by the search engine like a phrase that belongs in a certain order. Punctuation will influence how queries appear; disregard some periods and commas.

Google allows users to search for a specific site by typing "site:wikipedia.com images," which will only include pages in that domain. Many websites also have a search box on their very site, and often, that search feature is "powered by Google" and is referred to as a Programmable Search Engine. It is available to be embedded in any site a Web developer chooses. However, this "site" search method is useful when the developers have not embedded a search feature onto their website.

Most search engines, whether public or specific to a platform like searching through Windows File Explorer, can use the asterisk wildcard. On Google, an asterisk can be used instead of a word in the event a user knows some parts of a phrase but not all of it. Multiple wildcards can be used in a string, such as the following, which contains literal quotes since this is a phrase: "break me off a * of that * *." In this case, Google can be assisted in recognizing the position of the words, and the quotation marks instantiate that this is a linguistic phrase. Searching techniques can be used in conjunction with one another.

When searching for a thing that has a widely known common usage, but the search is meant to find a more obscure entity, using the minus sign can help guide the engine to better results. An example of this would be: "Daisy -flower." This search should effectively find people named Daisy and not show results for the common flower. These types of modifiers are simple enough to use but will greatly refine search results.

A more obscure effect of searching is to seek out all the webpages that have a link to a certain site on the page. Using this method, a user can effectively find where all a specific URL is being posted. Link searching shines some light on how search engines go about indexing webpages and the links they contain. However, one flaw in this is that some links have been intentionally shortened to look cleaner and easier to copy and paste. Also, some pages might have completely different links to the same page because some links are rerouted. Nonetheless, the following example would usually work for a site like

SoundCloud: "link:soundcloud.com/rolling-stone-official," which shows all the places where the Rolling Stones band has posted their SoundCloud link. Using site-based searching helps to outline the semantic interconnectedness by showing how closely traversable webpages really are. When researching a subject or trying to find an answer to a complex problem, it is a good idea to try to learn from various sources. Using Google's related modified works as such: "related:theverge.com," which displays all the pages related to the technologically focused news site *The Verge*.

People who search online can sometimes be stumped by the glob of results when all they want is a specific thing. For this example, someone is trying to find ebooks, but they can only find a certain book, *Dracula,* in .pdf when they want to find a version in .epub. An accurate and real query for this is to search "Dracula by Bram Stoker filetype:.epub," This search query results in several pages with a hotlink embedded in the actual Google results page. Be sure to be cautious when clicking on these hotlinks because they will immediately download the file, as opposed to opening a website.

Google has several built-in APIs (Application Programming Interfaces) that directly connect people with what they are attempting to find. One such is with the company The Weather Company, LLC. Searching a city and then the word weather will embed a weather forecast right into the Google results page. The query would look something simple like this: "Elizabeth City weather."

As many people know, Google is excellent at making conversions for measurements. "1,000ml to oz" is all a user needs to input to get an immediate result provided directly by

Google. Avoiding other unnecessary words is wise because it may negatively affect the engine's algorithms.

Another interesting and random feature of Google is it has a musical instrument tuner. Using this feature requires a microphone or a direct interface signal from an electric instrument to evaluate the signal and help a musician tune their instrument to the correct frequencies. A search engine combined with various helpful APIs helps to better gather information in the same place, which is extremely useful.

Something that makes the Web difficult to navigate through is dead links. Hyperlinks that fail to function act like dead-ends on the digital roads of the Internet. However, unlike real streets, dead links can be more similar to an entire road disappearing. Link rot is the denoted term for this type of Internet atrophy, and it lessens the cohesive robustness for which the Web is known. Almost everyone has read an article several years old or watched an obscure YouTube video, both of which had URLs that present an error 404 upon visiting or perhaps are even rerouted to a different location than the original link intended. Fortunately, many of these dead links can be resurrected, at least in the manner of being able to be viewed but not interacted with. The Wayback Machine can help with this conundrum. The Wayback Machine has been gaining significant popularity in the last several years, and it is a sort of website necromancer –or at least it can display webpages that no longer exist. The Web has seen billions of webpages come and go since its inception, and it is a real shame that many of those sites are lost forever, but that is the problem the Wayback Machine seeks to remedy. At the time of this writing, Wayback Machine touts that it can view more than

866 billion pages. The system functions as a search engine in its ability to index links to evaluate popularity and, thus, search result ranking for a now-dead page. Wayback Machine can be used as a search engine, but it also accepts URLs if the user knows the dead page they want to see.

How could a system still view pages that no longer exist? By snapshotting the page while it is in existence. In 1996, the Wayback Machine was created to begin the daunting project of archiving the Web, and the search engine has functioned extremely well given the amorphous structure of the Internet. The project did not go public until 2001, but it did so with an impressive catalog of 10 billion pages upon its debut. The Wayback Machine exists as a component of the Internet Archive, and its overarching goal is (somewhat obviously) archiving the Internet and its assets, so backup copies exist. Wayback Machine crawls the Web at certain intervals, and specific timestamped pages are saved and marked all the way down to the second they were archived. Unfortunately, Javascript and other elaborate methods of coding are difficult to archive; the Wayback Machine can primarily index simple HTML pages and struggles to save more elaborate visual components of websites, which can make certain archived pages unreadable and their images difficult to view. This leads to the problem that some more recent websites may not be as easy to back up because animations made by Javascript can make many parts of a website non-viewable after a copy is saved by the Machine. In January 2024, Wayback stored 99 petabytes of data, which is saved to special PetaBox rack storage units custom-designed and maintained by the Internet Archive's staff.

The most discerning participants of the Web are its users. An individual understanding what they are looking to find online and then pursuing that entity is the best way to navigate the Web without external forces having too much influence over their personal decision-making. There do not seem to be any individuals online –at least from the perspective of the algorithms that decide how to serve ads, YouTube videos, and Tweets. People online are categorized and determined to be similar, and then they are distributed the same dull, algorithmic content. However, more unique methods of searching allow individuals to find a more comfortable and unique experience online.

Chapter 7 – Conscientious Intermission

A rt is permittable and sociably acceptable chaos. Few artists are known to proliferate the general degradation of society. On the contrary, media like music and film explain negative aspects of society while also shining a light on more positive attributes. The free world greatly enjoys outlandish and somewhat bizarre practices. Digitalized art is created with pixels amidst variously exchanged communication, even amidst radio frequencies. So then, is the sound and sight of data undetectable? Indeed it is. What else can set someone free when searching higher? Did Maslow simply have a joke he wanted to tell over the course of a few hundred years? Were his victors not accomplished enough? Perhaps his winners of society were too accomplished to the point of tyranny. I do not know, but Maslow had ideas that stayed stern among people, and thus, the same blessed people congregate online to find what has washed up on the shore of the electric sea when looking to fulfill the highest tiers of Maslow's Hierarchy. Art (in its various forms) can be found online at a quantity and accessibility never before known.

Stephen Hawking is quoted in a British Telecom ad as saying, "For millions of years, mankind lived just like the animals. Then something happened which unleashed the power of our imagination. We learned to talk and we learned to listen. Speech has allowed the communication of ideas, enabling human beings to work together to build the impossible. Mankind's greatest achievements have come about by talking, and its greatest failures by not talking. It doesn't have to be like this. Our greatest hopes could become reality in the future. With the technology at our disposal, the possibilities are unbounded. All we need to do is make sure we keep talking."

I first heard Hawking's statement in the Pink Floyd song "Keep Talking," which only sampled, "It doesn't have to be like this." Then, in the following line of the song: "All we need to do is make sure we keep talking."

Hawking's assertion that communication is imperative to humanity's success or society's downfall if it is not instilled is a testament to the man's greatness. With the potential for elaborate and extensive communication on the Internet, it is no wonder that people knew that it would change the world, and it is still impacting the Earth and our future.

The Internet is humankind's most prolific conversation. We are able to converse with an extremely long past as a result of the extensive information archiving much of the Internet has permitted in numerous fields of science, literature, and other humanistic pursuits. The Web also enables us to converse with those who have since passed and to provide even more conversations about the future, which many forms of media are incapable of being that well documented. Ports 80 and 443 are a gentle storm of energy on an otherwise disagreeable rock. You would do well to find some signals that encourage you and ignore those that do not because the supply of both seems oddly endless and not always discernible. However, be sure not to show the fragility of your electronics and stand against hate and deceit, which both come in abundance on what is sent and received in this weird and intangible means of communication.

Conversations are easy to find on the Internet. Unfortunately, some of these conversations are not terribly well structured, such as the comment section on YouTube. General bickering and tit-for-tat remarks have become a cornerstone of being online, which is unfortunate because this technology is conducive to significantly more than overly emotional arguing. Most spats result from a lack of understanding from either arguing party and interestingly enough, these arguments exist as an exchange of a few comments. Emotions and curtness can destroy otherwise productive talks. Online, people stand behind figurative walls and lob well-made nonsense at their rival's walls, only to have these ideas smash into the barricade and fall broken on the ground. Discussions require a significantly greater amount of patience than our current Web allows for in most cases.

Long-form narrative discussions between people (which are frequently not a bad thing but a good way of establishing truths and identifying perspectives resulting from experience) are just as they are named; they take a long time. Engaging in a conversation that lasts a little while creates a relationship with a person, even if it is simple and brief. Relationships tend to either cease or improve over time. Reading a comment and rapidly responding is not a positive relationship. The longer a conversation continues, the more familiar the conversationalists become with one another, and people tend to like people they regularly speak with much better than strangers. Being online is tough for that reason: everyone you meet is nearly a stranger. However, because of the various interest groups and sites that cater to realms of hobbies, people have a starting point to talk with one another. Furthermore, typing things at someone is much easier than speaking verbally with a furious and cursing rhetoric; most people do not behave with animosity when out in public. There is a different kind of rage that seems to exist solely on the Internet.

Understanding dichotomies and how to balance such strange circumstances as two ideas holding truth is very important when it comes to using the Web. The amount of information out there is extremely overwhelming, and unfortunately, it is difficult for someone to know what is accurate and what is not. No matter who creates different webpages or writes news articles, it can be difficult to confirm what their motives are or if they are even accurate because much of the information online does not come with multiple verifiable sources. Spending time online can present an onslaught of information to a user. However, some of those pieces of information can help a person substantially in bringing about joy. Music, film, art, and literature are all prolific online. These artistic formats of expression and entertainment are getting buried, perhaps in part by bots and spammers on social media.

As a writer, I would not be able to read nearly as much as I do if it were not for organizations like the Gutenberg Project and other online libraries and subscription services that distribute books. Ebook sales become more popular every day, and online retailers that sell paper books are as popular as ever. Additionally, information formatted into a book is very enjoyable for me to consume because I prefer the pace of learning that reading presents (perhaps you feel the same way), as opposed to more subjects being presented in a two-hour film, which can leave out details. However, the variety of media formats helps greatly in learning, and as someone who has had Internet access since I was about seven years old, I feel blessed to be a child of the digital world that exists online, and many people of my generation are the first to be engaged with the Web at a young age, for better or for worse. Personally, I would not have it any other way.

Focusing on pragmatism will help you succeed online and not be a victim of the mild torture that the overwhelming noise of the Web can present to a person. I always try to consider the value of the information I find online. As far as the pleasures of the Internet, I also attempt (sometimes not successfully) to moderate how often I play games or mindlessly stare at YouTube while exciting but hollow topics flash across my computer screen. We seem to live in an era of addiction –where addictions are often glazed over and even laughed at. Habits are extremely difficult to alter, but wild success does stem from self-control and habitual changes. Unfortunately for many addicts, they do not quickly realize they are addicted, but harm continues to besiege their psyche as they helplessly and unknowingly falter in life. The digital imitation of society we are all able to take part in needs to be engaged with cautiously.

• • • •

The Internet has developed quite a reputation over the years, and people approach this machine with different ideologies. Many aspects of the online world are fantastic and can benefit people in any pursuit they wish to pursue –because surely there is enough information available to help a person succeed in this strange world. Meanwhile, there is much evil online that preys on people's minds and ekes out as much dopamine as possible, so they are left to wander around the tangible world upset with it as though their offline existence were a hard jail cell.

Many technological philosophers have spoken about their ideas regarding the Web.

"The Internet was supposed to homogenize everyone by connecting us all. Instead, what it's allowed is silos of interest." a quote by the author and businessman Seth Godin detailing the seclusion and bigotry the Web can coax out of a person.

"We are all now connected by the Internet, like neurons in a giant brain."

Hawking also discussed collectivism. Ultimately, Hawking's idea here shows a more microcosmic view of the Internet, while alternatively, Godin describes the islands of ideas similar people live on. Dichotomies are everywhere on the Web, and Hawking, in this case, appears to have a more positive and synergistic view of the Web, while Godin is more disdainful.

After too much interaction with people, whether that be in a crowd or reading comments and things online, there quickly comes a point when I want to completely disengage. On that platform, people are given voices who have no business commenting on a subject because their bias follows them around like an angry shadow. Voiced opinions swirl all around my mind when I dabble in social platforms for too long. However, that definitely helped me understand logical dichotomies much better and filter the good out of the chaos of the Web. Multiple things can be true at once; there is balance in clear thinking, but our always interconnected devices are disrupting that, and individualism is burning under the sun of egalitarianism that prevails online.

Douglas Adams has said, "Don't believe anything you read on the net. Except this. Well, including this, I suppose."

The man who wrote *The Hitchhiker's Guide to the Galaxy* was well prepared to understand something so absurd. Everyone has their own ideals that they bring to the Internet (for some odd reason). Frequently, people just want to get into a good fight online and take out some anger on their fellow virtual man. People only believe what they want to, but time wins many battles of logic. Seeking information requires balance. Sometimes, relying on your own instincts is the best decision, as opposed to seeking out convoluted ideas on the Web that may not fit your situation. Groupthink can absolutely squash an individual's ideas, even though these ideas do not contribute to the betterment of you as an individual, and that is one of the Internet's most important causes: individualism.

Chapter 8 – Intimate Intranets

Intranets are networks that are partitioned inside organizations and businesses. Intranets are not publicly accessible networks. Many intranets have moderated access to the Internet, but an intranet is a network in and of itself and frequently consists of a combination of physical and cloud machines working in conjunction. Organizations need to use devices like NAS (Network Access Storage) and their more expensive alternatives, SAN (Storage Area Network) boxes, to store vast quantities of data physically on a rack. Frequently, on a business's intranet, their storage needs to be local due to the vast size of the storage, as well as to keep its potentially proprietary data secure. Data can also be stored in an intranet topology that is privately connected to the cloud, such as how SharePoint is often configured. When a connection departs from the local intranet, it may be a virtual private connection that is encrypted and never traverses the public Internet, making it far more secure, even though it does access a point at a different network location. However, not all intranet-to-Internet connections require extremely secure connections with elaborate encryption. The networks comprising a business's interior network can be monitored by SIEMs (Security Information and Event Management) that evaluate network traffic and systems shared among employees, like Jira, an elaborate team management platform used by organizations.

An extranet is when someone, like a business associate or customer, accesses an intranet remotely, which is again connected by the Internet or VPC (Virtual Private Connection) to maintain a secure encrypted connection. Enterprise private networks connect intranets that are geographically separate, which helps to gather resources together, better access files, and help team members communicate.

• • • •

A network is defined as two or more devices that are somehow connected and capable of communicating together. In some ways, devices like desktop computers and phones are networks in and of themselves because there are numerous electronics on their motherboard that communicate together to enable different features of a device. Solid-state drives have their own processor, and GPUs (Graphics Processing Unit) are a daughterboard in their own right. As computer components become more advanced, so will network communication. On a desktop motherboard, there is typically a CPU, GPU, RAM, and a network interface controller (often referred to as a NIC), not to mention several other common components. The CPU acts as the manager of the system and designates computational tasks to different devices, all of which work together and exchange data. External GPUs (eGPUs) are becoming more popular, and they are connected to a computer via Thunderbolt or USB-C (Universal Serial Bus C, which is the third iteration). Potentially, in the future, as networking capabilities improve, computers may be able to remotely attach devices like GPUs and RAM to borrow performance, and some cloud services already share virtualized whole computers for high-performance tasks. Those connected devices sound a lot like a network. However, to make matters more clear, most networks are connected via ethernet cables or radio frequencies, both of which are the responsibility of a NIC.

The Internet of Things is a broad look at how everyday devices are communicating with each other and the Internet. The number of network-attached devices people use in their homes is quietly exploding. Collectively, the devices people use on a daily basis form a more intimate experience for people. Individuals are forming personal networks with their devices, and they themselves are becoming similar to the CPU as the basis for managing this new network. The most important device in this intimate intranet is its human user, which shepherds these reckless and vulnerable devices.

In an emergency situation, such as when a device becomes infected with malware on an organization's network, there is a big red button moment when the organization's network professionals have to make the decision to pull the plug and disconnect the firewall from the Internet and outside world. Firewalls act as the exterior barrier of a network; if the firewall is disconnected (physically or virtually, in the case of cloud infrastructure), the entire network no longer has Internet access, which prevents any threat actors from remotely doing harm to the network as pulling the plug would sever their connection. This is accomplished by denying all traffic from the Internet to the firewall or, in the context of more simple configurations, unplugging the ethernet cable from the firewall that ultimately leads to the Internet service provider. Once the network is disconnected from the outside world, it remains an offline network: an intranet. Computers can still transmit data, such as files, or begin remote desktop interactions with other devices on the network, but the intranet is now on an island.

Confidentiality, integrity, and availability (CIA, or CIA Triad, but no, not that CIA) is one of the most beloved principles of all network security professionals and exists as a trio of dichotomies –perhaps a trichotomy. CIA has to be balanced for a network to work most effectively. A network with extremely high availability will inevitably be the least secure because a network experiences downtimes to update and make protective configurations that cannot be completed online. Meanwhile, a network with significantly too much integrity will have so many safeguards in place that communicating could become cumbersome, such as when using a system that verifies that emails are from legitimate employees. Despite this practice often being effective, it can also slow down workflow.

Intranets that are not connected to the Internet are the most secure networks. Routinely used electronics with network accessibility like desktops, laptops, phones, gaming devices, tablets, televisions, wireless access points, aquarium thermostats, printers, speakers, refrigerators, and many other devices make up personal networks. Most of these devices do not need to be connected to the Internet, as keeping cheese sticks and tortillas cold, quite notably, does not require an Internet connection. The safest network is one that is not connected to the outside world, and devices that do not require an Internet connection definitely should not have one. A strong wall only needs to lose a few bricks for it to become insecure. Cheaply engineered devices and even extensively developed devices all have vulnerabilities. Vulnerabilities get progressively worse as updates stop being released because the companies that make these devices cannot be bothered to continue pushing out updates, or they may consider that specific device deprecated, i.e., they gave up on maintaining a product because they want to sell new stuff. Open-source scripts in Python, PowerShell, and other languages allow script kiddies to easily launch attacks against flimsy IoT devices. Many consumers are not aware they need to update obscure devices like PC (Personal Computer) drivers or wireless access points, and such a process can be made too difficult to achieve by the original developers.

Many IoT objects should have controls put in place so that they cannot access the Internet. Contrarily, the more harmful outcome would be if the Internet were to contact them. Preventing illicit remote access is more easily said than done. Practically all devices can be jailbroken. Jailbreaking is the act of manipulating a device to complete different tasks than originally planned by the developer.

A popular realm of study in cybersecurity is jailbreaking video game consoles. The first goal in exploiting a console that has not yet had any known vulnerabilities is to run unsigned code. Once a researcher can run code, they can install an operating system (nearly all of which are Linux-based operating systems), and they can then use the console as something that resembles a Linux desktop that can run all kinds of applications.

In the case of criminal hacking, similar types of device hijacking can take place with the intent to steal information, ransom the network for profit, or destroy the network outright. All devices can be jailbroken; it is simply a matter of time before a device becomes capable of being totally exploited.

Most devices should not be connected to the Internet because it is dangerous out in the wilderness of the Web. Devices would work just as well if they could stay on an offline network, but that is difficult to implement because if a computer can connect to a wireless access point, it is difficult to contain it to only an offline intranet, and most developers do not seem to consider this as an option. The Web manipulates both people and IoT products, and people would do well to be more conscious of what their personal network is bumping shoulders with because all devices can be scanned for vulnerabilities, payloads delivered, and control can then be assumed.

The first micro-intranet that formed a motley crew of network devices was the small-scale network of a PC, printer, and landline phone. In this case, the telephone would not be able to have any kind of network communication between itself and the PC or printer because telephones do not have an IP and therefore do not communicate in the Internet Protocol standard, even though back in the day telephones and PCs shared the phone line. So, technically, landline telephones are a different category of network device. In the days of dial-up, these two devices could not simultaneously connect to the phone network or the Internet. Of course, in modern computing, dial-up is no longer popular among consumers, and there are a plethora of IoT devices. Now, it is common for regular consumers to have numerous devices to fulfill their wants and needs, and collectively, these devices make up a household intranet. However, many households do not technically have enough devices to compare to, say, a business with dozens of devices in use that are managed by a switch. The IoT trend seems to suggest that households will soon have enough technology connecting to their wireless access point, and more care will need to be taken to secure all of these devices with easily defeated security. Your fridge may be in more danger than you realize.

Chapter 9 - Entertainment

Video live streaming on the Web has been around since the early 1990s, but the concept of a live broadcast in any format has been around even longer. In 1881, Théâtrophone began offering a subscription-based service that broadcasted live theater and opera shows to subscribers' phone lines where they would listen in. The Théâtrophone was extremely cutting edge for its time, and the fact that the broadcasters ran their signal on telephone lines rather than radio (radio technology would not have been capable of such a broadcast at the time) is somewhat similar to a network topology in its most rudimentary form, although of course its users could not send anything, they could only receive the broadcast from the theater shows Several decades later, the first live radio broadcast began on November 2, 1920, in Pittsburgh when Westinghouse Electric and Manufacturing Company broadcasted the Harding vs. Cox presidential debate. Both of these early uses of networking, phone lines, and radio signal broadcasting would begin an era that prevails today, that being the era of live media.

People naturally enjoy live entertainment because it is more engaging to know that the spectacle is happening just as they listen or watch.

Radio signal broadcasting (one example of which is Wi-Fi), wire cables, and fiber optic technological advancement correspondingly act as three of the most important factors in the improvement of Internet latency and communications as a whole. Mobile broadcasting of sound and video followed the initial means of broadcasting, which utilized a high-speed wired connection that was only first available from a desktop computer and is frequently assisted by fiber optic connections or a high-upload speed connection.

Early phone lines were made of iron and steel; it was not until 1881 when copper strands were twisted together to form what would become modern phone lines, which had a massive impact on the field of networking and communications technology because copper is one the most important elements used in electronics, especially early in communications development where these lines were the only means of connecting phones.

Generally, people enjoy partaking in a live experience, even when they are unable to attend an event such as boxing, which was one of the most popular sports in the world beginning in 1921, which marked its official organized group with the creation of The National Boxing Association, despite the sport being popular for centuries. Radio and boxing thrived in tandem as their official creation occurred nearly at the same time. Radio broadcasts of boxing matches were incredibly popular until the 1950s, when the introduction of televisions brought the accompaniment of images to the previously audio-only experience of a fight.

Skipping ahead to the late 1990s when the term livestream began, a livestream is a broadcast online that features both sound and video. Various websites would host live streams, but it was not a super popular form of entertainment.

In 2007, Justin Kan, Emmett Shear, Michael Seibel, and Kyle Vogt began the website Justin TV, which was one of the earliest platforms that allowed anyone to create a live broadcasted audio and video stream, which is usually referred to simply as streaming. Justin Kan began Justin TV as a way to stream his life 24/7, hence the name of the platform. From justin.tv's inception in 2007 to 2014, the term "livestream" appeared 27 times as frequently in Google Books corpus as can be seen on Google's Ngram viewer.

In 2011, Twitch became justin.tv's separated home for streams featuring video games, and in 2014, the entire platform was rebranded as Twitch. Some livestreams feature a feed from a camera, while others commonly display the live feed of a video game being played, which is popular on the streaming platform Twitch, now owned by Amazon. Millions of people visit livestreaming sites, and it certainly seems as though people have a strong affinity to live media. Naturally, live television broadcasts have existed since the broadcast of the Berlin Olympics on August 14, 1936, but anyone is able to stream on the Web, and it is as cheap as ever, especially when compared to how a television channel would broadcast live to cable or satellite TV providers.

Most livestreams contain a live text chat feature alongside the stream in real-time. The chat is by active viewers and is how the streamer engages with their viewers, as well as how the viewership converses among themselves with text and emotes. The conversational narrative that chats along with the stream puts a special twist on this form of entertainment.

Livestreaming serves an elaborately varied collection of content from pornography all the way to NASA (National Aeronautics and Space Administration) spacecraft launches. During the last solar eclipse in North America, NASA featured a livestream from Niagara Falls in New York. Some streamers broadcast their daily lives on Twitch, and the streamer Frank Taylor's Lifecast (also under the handle FranknCats) has streamed quite regularly for over a decade, having started in 2009. In recent years, the National Football League has had Thursday Night Football games streamed to Twitch via Prime Video, which is proof of streaming coming full circle from its beginnings as an amateur way to broadcasting, now including massive media companies that are also participating in the same technology.

Livestream websites have rapidly increased in popularity since 2007, and that has mostly to do with technological accessibility to both stream and view streams, which takes significant bandwidth. In order to stream at the highest possible quality, which is usually near 1080p, although 1440p is in beta testing on some platforms, a streamer needs to have high-speed Internet, and before Justin TV in 2007, it was quite costly and rare to have such good quality Internet access. Now, the average Internet connection in many places is likely able to broadcast at a viewable quality. The other main components required in streaming are, of course, a computer and a camera, the latter of which has improved rampantly, and cheap video cameras are readily available that can film in high definition. Streamers that film themselves live in public stream from a smartphone, which again, was not capable of having fast enough Internet via a mobile connection, and smartphones capable of processing filming while simultaneously uploading the video feed and audio were not cheap enough to be practical for most consumers streaming for fun. Today, Twitch is worth approximately $45 billion, while Kick, another streaming site, is worth $60 million. Livestreaming has become somewhat lucrative for these sites based on tips and subscriptions, but the advertisements streaming services make from their viewers is where they profit.

When discussing online videos, it is impossible to ignore the juggernaut that is YouTube. YouTube began its streaming services in April 2011 and is one of the few sites that allow both livestreaming and standard video uploads. Both Kick and Twitch have VODs (Video on Demand), a term used to describe past broadcasts that are archived for people to watch later, but typically livestreaming sites do not have direct video uploads.

Interactions with the chat, as well as other streams, are popular on livestreams, even in streams that maintain an audience of hundreds of thousands. Numerous gaming tournaments featuring esports games such as Counter-Strike 2, Overwatch 2, League of Legends, and many others have been broadcast on Twitch. For several years, television subscriptions have declined, and many people have expected live programming to be replaced by channels on the Web or phone apps. Livestreaming is slowly becoming part of that with sports broadcasts, both video-game sports and traditional sports like American football.

Many forms of media are now available exclusively online. Online-only platforms can be both good and bad. Some forms of software as a service are effectively scams, and some video game companies have been sued for launching a game that subsequently went offline a few years after being released without stating that such a thing was going to happen. Less negative ideas persist about movies and TV show subscription services, but the fact remains that members are paying for a privilege and not a product. This controversy is one that will likely get worse before it improves.

Music services like Spotify and SoundCloud have grown rampantly in the last decade, and Spotify in 2024 has a net worth of $60.67 billion, an incredible number considering they only sell subscriptions and not palpable products. According to Spotify's website, their platform is home to over 100 million songs, 6 million podcast titles, and 350 thousand podcasts. Due to technologically advancing Internet speeds, Spotify offers up to 320 kbps audio streaming, and the company plans to add lossless audio in the near future.

For many people, the Web exists for the sole purpose of entertainment, which is not a bad way to utilize it. Plenty of enticing forms of engaging media can be found online.

Chapter 10 – Inquiring Minds

The World Wide Web has greatly reorganized education, both in the broad sense of how information spreads and also in the traditional structure of schooling at all levels. Digital chatter on copper lines means so much now, perhaps more than it ever has. In today's world, accessing information online is a requirement, even for elementary school children. While in higher education, complete trade curriculums and college degree programs are available entirely online, forgoing the requirements that a person be near a physical campus. One of the best descriptions of the Internet is that it is an elaborate network of information, which is great news for those who want to learn. In the early days of the Internet, simple webpages hosted things that would be difficult to find elsewhere. Many of these sites have been in existence for over three decades now, and their foundational influence is strong.

What do people search for on the Internet? Well, people have searched for a litany of zany and peculiar things online and will continue to do so with even more randomness. Navigating through the search results of a query displays many sites like Quora displaying all the bizarre and fairly inappropriate questions people have inquired to the abyss that is the Internet. Some questions would be more appropriate for a medical professional, psychologist, or well-regarded legal team, but ports 80 and 443 are home to many a desperate inquiry. Google is used in this instance because it is the most popular search engine in the US and has easily accessible data about the search engine's use, but it should be noted that Duck

Duck Go is a great search engine to use when looking for less well-known subjects or when Google has censored sites from its search results, despite often doing so without appropriate grounds.

One of the most popular questions Google was asked is the prompt "What is my ip." Considering most Internet users do not care what their IP is, the quantity of this query is likely from automated scripts that need to affirm what their IP is, and IT (Information Technology) professionals frequently search the phrase for practical purposes. Additionally, asking "What is my ip" with any other structure is grammatically difficult. "What is my ip address" is also the fifteenth most popular question.

"What to watch" is a pleasant and simplistic question that is the second most popular search query that Google receives. This query is oddly vague. What is the Internet for, if not mostly entertainment? Frequently, Google searches seem to be the start of a conversation and exist as a small window into people's lives. Google searches are people's ideas that bubble to the surface of their minds until their curiosity overtakes them, and they type their thoughts into the Omnibox.

"How many weeks are in a year" is the third most popular search, and the top ten is full of similar mundane questions. There are fifty-two weeks in a year, just as there are fifty-two playing cards in a deck. Although not particularly interesting, consulting a search engine for this question would be much faster than the alternative of manually counting how many weeks are in a year on a calendar. Simple questions are easily answered with search engines, and the perplexing idea persists that before search engines, finding information took a multitude of times longer than it does now, or alternatively, those questions would have never been answered for the asker.

The 38th most popular search is "How much house can I afford" which is a rather serious question to look to Google for an answer. A search engine is an excellent means to receive numerous and elaborate responses for a question, and having diverse responses is a good way to approach the truth. Dozens of questions need to be answered before determining what a home buyer should pay for a house, so such an important question will probably not be well-answered by Google. People often search the Web because they do not have better resources on hand.

Maslow's hierarchy of needs is a concept introduced by the American psychologist Abraham Maslow in 1943 in the paper "A Theory of Human Motivation." The concept is displayed as a pyramid, where the most vital needs of a human being are located at the bottom, while more social and philosophical needs are at the top of the pyramid. An interesting way of finding out the common issues a person contends with is by researching what people search online for; where do most of the questions Internet users ask fall on Maslow's hierarchy? This evaluation shows how important search engines have become to people's psychological and, in some cases, physiological needs. Search results can give a glimpse into what issues regular Internet users are facing and what conceptualized level of need they are trying to fulfill, ranging from healthcare questions to searches for local fast food.

Normal people are becoming more directly connected to search engines, and this is influencing their decision-making. On average, people do three to four Web searches a day, according to Worldmetrics. The AI language models and other algorithms that help search engines function, especially Bing and Google, which have the most capable AI algorithms, are potent tools that are new additions to how engines function. Search engines affect how people think because these couriers of the vast Internet can answer any question, causing engines to change what searchers learn. Modern technology, and today's society in general, is frequently described as on-demand and instant gratification is available via not only the Internet but other technologies that smartphones have brought to the masses. People walk around every day with a wealth of knowledge holstered in their pockets. Smartphones are no longer just telephones. Smartphones can now act as notebooks, cameras, maps, and numerous other devices, but a direct connection to the Web is the most significant result of modern phones.

Norm Macdonald had a joke in one of his stand-up routines:

"You know, it was back then, I remember if you wanted to take a picture you would use a camera. Not a telephone. As a matter of fact, if you used a telephone people would look at you odd."

Smartphones have become modern society's most intimate electronic companion. People take their phones everywhere they go and tell their phones strange problems and secrets they would never say to anyone else when they Google things and take notes. This is all very unusual to ponder. Many people feel lost and despondent at some point in their lives. Perhaps they do not realize all their solutions, and indeed the whole world's solutions, are on the Internet (good luck finding them). This is the reason why search engines are so vital to society; search engines are the fastest way to acquire important information that can be used to figure something out, a true weapon against the chaos of modern life.

Search engines enable anyone and everyone to access information online. One very important purveyor and protector of information online is the Internet Archive. Internet Archive is a file-sharing repository, and the mission of this nonprofit organization is to safely store and distribute ebooks, documents, software, audio files, and much more. Not dissimilar from other file-sharing websites, Internet Archive does distribute copyrighted content, which has resulted in Internet Archive having to appear in court several times. However, the burden lies on the copyright owner to report their content on Internet Archive as being their intellectual property, such as a musician initiating a claim that their music (which is likely being sold legitimately on other platforms) is being made available on Internet Archive for free. Most creators cannot be bothered to stop people from posting their copyrighted material online, and stopping people from uploading items would be extremely difficult for certain popular items like ebooks or videos as they are uploaded in dozens of different places on the Archive's immense library.

Internet Archive operates in a gray area because of the fact that they are a nonprofit and do not sell the files people download from their digital library, although most of the files the Archive hosts are legally able to be distributed just as physical libraries can distribute materials. Additionally, Internet Archive has an exemption from DMCA because the site maintains archived data that could otherwise be lost;

archiving has always been the chief mission of the organization. The Internet Archive will likely continue to have legal interactions, but it will always store and distribute millions of files that are permitted to be distributed, such as items with expired copyrights.

· · · ·

Most of the searches people make through a search engine, or the questions they ask a search engine, are pragmatic and relatable utterances of the human experience. What a person searches online reveals a significant amount about their personality and character. There is a considerable amount of concern about what companies do with people's personal information, and as mentioned, what is more revealing than someone's search history? Companies keep close track of what consumers do and frequently use this information to target the person with catered advertisements they are likely to click. Due to security breakdowns, the same companies also have data breaches, which causes personally identifiable information to become available on the dark web. The fact that search engines have more information about individuals than they may even realize about themselves is not good. Several countries have taken action to limit corporate overreach. Still, there does not seem to be a specific tangible way to stop corporations from storing information about a person's activities online, such as what webpages they visit and displaying ads to things other people viewed that have similar Web activity.

Despite the massive practical applications the Web provides, there are also damaging psychological aspects to using the Web. Overuse of social media is synonymous with dependency and depression. The social interactions on social network sites can be overly stimulating by connecting people to a large number of people. However, being able to compare oneself with as many people as the breadth of the Internet holds is where the depression factor begins to make sense. The vague connections people have with one another can also cause a lack of gratification, like an addicted gambler refusing to stop spinning the wheel, eternally seeking a win amidst the minuscule odds of success. Negative psychological aspects of being online are formally referred to as problematic Internet use. Limiting both the amount of time and nature of activities completed online is necessary in this day and age of the nearly all-encompassing Internet of Things. Internet use is becoming difficult to prevent; almost everyone spends time online today. It is hard to escape.

The Internet is an abstract metaphor for human life. Some of the things found online show the agonizing struggles that people undergo in their attempt to survive formatted into podcasts. Other things are digitally encapsulated items of art and beauty found in music online.

Due to the dopamine feedback loop, people struggle with social media addiction, and these platforms only benefit from this type of addiction because it garners their applications more use, increasing ad revenue. If someone can begin a sort of macabre game, they will continue playing if there is a potential reward even though the reward is not tangible and very irregular, which promotes a guise of rarity and value. Rarity is good in a monkey-brain type of mindset, even if the rare reward is practically useless. If there is an unlikely chance of something happening, and an addicted person thinks they need to try harder to find success, leading to exhaustion. They cannot realize the odds of finding gratification in social media are so close to being nonexistent that putting considerable amounts of time into such a platform is wasteful at best and psychologically damaging at worst. However, some of the connections online are prudent for one's social health. Not all explorations online are gratifying, whether for entertainment, friendship, or learning. All Internet users would do well to understand how staunchly addicted modern people have become to flimsy online pleasures. The Internet should be used for good, and a focus needs to be on using effective searching rather than looping metaphorical digital gambling that vehemently wastes time and leaves lasting impacts on people's brains after significant time spent online.

Considering the state of the Internet of Things, nearly all popular electronics are connected to the Internet. Logging in using similar credentials, such as logging into a Google account on a PC, video game console, or smartphone, causes a huge amount of data to be stored about a person's activities. Due to the breadth of situations these devices are used in, a hacker would find it easier than ever to breach one of these devices and steal a multitude of information about someone. In the past, social security numbers, credit card numbers, and bank accounts were the main targets of hackers who typically attempted to steal this information so they could then turn around and resell masses of data on the dark web. Nowadays, a person can lose more than just money or even their identity; they are losing important data relevant to their daily activities. Because of the amount of personal data devices contain, falsely incriminating someone on circumstantial evidence should theoretically be as easy as ever. For example, tax fraud. Everyone (supposedly) pays taxes; what if a person's search history was acquired and all the odd questions they ever searched about tax laws were shown as evidence against them? In reality, the person may be innocent, but the strange yet natural curiosity of people can appear to be falsely incriminating, and at some point, this data is going to be used in a court of law. Law enforcement does not hesitate to demand that technology companies allow them access to suspected criminal's devices. Long gone are the days when an individual could buy cocaine online from their smart fridge without being found out.

Privacy has been argued for and supported by security professionals for years. As a person's own database becomes a more tangible codex stored by corporations, from advertisement distributors to grocery stores, privacy will only ever become a more important concept. Ignoring or disregarding privacy is foolhardy, and no matter a person's guilt, companies often mishandle their customers' data. No one would give their Internet usage data away if they knew it could be litigiously used against them. As mentioned previously, data can be easily manipulated to appear differently than it really is in order to disparage someone's reputation, and data breaches have proven that many of these companies that store customer data are not handling the data securely.

• • • •

The all-encompassing nature of the Internet has allowed people to gain a new kind of independence from traditional stores. Food, clothing, and even real estate can be purchased online. People are looking to the Internet to fulfill their hierarchy of needs. Some aspects of that fact are harmful, while others may be more positive. Friendships and other various social relationships flourish online. The social groups that began on platforms like Web forums have spread to become even more elaborate on social networking applications such as Discord, which is an entirely virtualized community. The Internet has greatly helped people fulfill stages of their own personal Maslow's hierarchy. The community platform Discord allows for voice and video communication but also can be considered the current apex of what an online forum can be, with text, pictures, videos, and music shared among a server's participants. Although most physiological needs are beyond the scope of what online stores can offer, anyone can certainly buy food, clothing, and some components of shelter, like building materials. Moving further up the pyramid to human safety needs, people can work entirely online and at least gain knowledge to better their safety, although that is obviously not as practically helped by the Internet.

The social tier of the hierarchy complicates how people interact on the Internet, but perhaps that is simply the nature of relationships. Relationships between people are extremely complicated, and the social credit between people is often not an evenly exchanged currency. Social media is known to be addictive for this reason: people constantly seek gratification to fulfill their social needs when online, and it is all for the worse that quantifiable numbers are shown for posts such as how Tweets are given thumbs up and retweeted. Being a loser is now quantifiable, or so the Internet would have us believe.

The fourth level of Maslow's hierarchy focuses on esteem and a person's ideas about themself. Confidence, which is typically a result of accomplishment, is the core concept of this tier. Receiving gratification for an achievement online is commonplace nowadays, but perhaps the most important aspect of this pursuit is the desire to be unique. Despite the Internet's ability to make anyone feel extremely insecure due to the abundance of children who can rapidly calculate limits in calculus and easily do double-backflips before deadlifting seven hundred pounds, the Internet is likely the best place in the world to be unique. The creativity that stems from the Web's ability to view interpersonal connections on this extremely vast network is incredible. Digitization of different art forms is prolific online. There seems to be an almost infinite amount of artwork, music, and hobbies people pursue and post about online. These more lofty art forms achieve a substantial amount for a person's psyche.

The top level of Maslow's pyramid is peculiar to consider in the context of an Internet-connected society. No matter who is being discussed, self-actualization in this top realm of needs is the most difficult to achieve, and there is some conflicting information about what a member of society should be like at the upper echelon of need. However, as Maslow's hierarchical ideas reach higher, so do the requirements for creativity, morality, and importance to become more evident. The information and increased capability online engagement provides a person appears to considerably help anyone fulfill more complex goals of esteem and self-actualization, which is a staple of a mentally healthy person. Unfortunately, the interactions people have with the Web are complex, and people

can be firmly helped or severely harmed by their Internet
habits.

Chapter 11 – Intermittent Reward

Intermittent reinforcement and intermittent reward are important to understand in general, but even more so in the context of how spending time on the Web influences people. The psychologist B.F. Skinner was the first to coin the term intermittent reinforcement in his essay "Reinforcement Today," published in *American Psychologist* in 1958. The reward portion of this idea is the positive stimulus that follows after an activity, which reinforces the idea that doing such a thing is good. However, for the strongest impact on a person, the reward is given irregularly. An example of why this happens is high-level competition. When playing a game, people feel more engaged with challenging games. That same person would quickly become disinterested if they very easily won the reward every time. People are often subversively affected by this mechanism, and its powerful nature can cause unintended intermittent reinforcement that sways how people behave.

Most modern apps are structured to further the mechanism of intermittent reinforcement to entice people to use the platforms more. When an app resembles a game, people will want to play with it. The massive number of people app users witness on apps like Instagram, X, and YouTube also gives the guise of a community, which implies that a user should also engage in these apps. People enjoy games and competitions, even when competing in games that have very hollow rewards and almost no long-term benefits. Nonetheless, people become extremely attached to these systems.

Internet addiction is when a person spends a significant enough amount of time engaging with the Internet that their life begins to suffer as a result. Like with most addictions, the person may not recognize the extent of the irrational decisions they are making because of the inherent habits that become deeply rooted in their personality over time. Many addictions occur in loops, such as when a firm desire is satiated by a stimulus. In this case, the stimulus is something on the Internet, such as playing a video game or engaging in social media; both of these tasks are not intrinsically harmful; it is only by addiction that these engagements turn into ensnaring life-altering problems. Intermittent reinforcement is at the core of why many people's habits become more self-destructive. Intermittent reinforcement is one of the best methods for maximizing effort (one of Skinner's key findings) from an individual, which will lead to exhaustion.

The concept of Internet addiction (as with much mental illness) is controversial and, in some cases, may stem from other behavioral disorders that are unresolved. Anxiety and depression play up dependencies in general, and the world online is an apparent escape for these predisposed people. Everything becomes even more muddled when considering some Internet use is practically mandatory in modern day-to-day lives, which is completely different than other addictions like drug dependency, where complete abstinence from the substance is a common treatment.

Unfortunately, the same potentially harmful mechanisms that exist online also benefit many Web-adjacent companies, such as video games. Everyone has seen the same cheap advertisements that describe a mobile game as being addictive

–as though that were a good thing. The intent of games (video games or traditional games like sports) is to engage in a struggle that is intermittently awarded with success. Success can be manifested in various forms of reward, such as winning a match in Counter-Strike or winning a hand in Texas hold'em, the latter of which can elicit an extreme emotional response because money is being risked. Activities do not necessarily need to be positive (like giving a dog a treat after it performs its trick). Some stimuli can be uncomfortable. People with issues managing their anger gain an affinity for the hot flush of anger that results from something happening. Excitement, which is not far from anger, can be an addictive response at the end of a behavioral loop. Sitting in stand-still traffic may elicit anger from someone. During the next few instances of this mundane annoyance happening, it may turn into a habit that continues to occur without logical reason.

Danger is fun. Discipline is difficult to hold onto in today's culture, and many people simply are not able to stay focused while on the Web of instantaneous pleasure. Discipline is an investment, which is abstractly a prediction of the future, and that is extremely tough (and sometimes impossible) to conceive for many people, especially when they are anxious and depressed.

Chapter 12 - An Adventure on the Internet

In terms of accessing literature on the Internet, Project Gutenberg is an honorable organization that freely shares ebooks online. All of the ebooks Project Gutenberg distributes are in the public domain, and the site has thousands of classic and iconic books. Project Gutenberg is the oldest digital library in existence. It was founded in 1971 when the organization's founder, Michael S. Hart, made a digital copy of the United States Declaration of Independence. After that event, Hart began the ambitious goal of creating digital copies of 10,000 of the most popular books so that they could be freely distributed to anyone. The organization's name is a reference to the inventor Johannes Gutenberg, and Hart's goals are intended to follow in the footsteps of the great inventor's press. The volunteers create digital books by typing or scanning the contents of books. Furthering the efforts of the Gutenberg Project, CV (Computer Vision) AI models have helped greatly in creating ebooks from physical books that only exist in that format. CV models can translate images to ebooks when scanning physical books. Unlike other file hosting sites, Gutenberg issues their ebooks with a license that explains the publication belongs to the public domain and that it may be distributed.

The Internet is a strange place with no shortage of bizarre content. Many of the things you can do on the Web are a far cry from reading a book.

Digital adventures are easy to go on amidst the vast networks that comprise the Internet. The Internet is the digitization of society, but it has less authority and enforcement than its real-life counterpart. Shared concepts that have been created by people are encapsulated online and are slowly contributing to a new system of human memory that can be accessed by anyone online. If someone has a question, it can likely be answered by the wealth of knowledge that is at their fingertips when using a phone or computer. With an ever-growing array of information, organizing that data is important, thus revealing the necessity of search engines because their ability to find things stems from their indexing of the Internet.

The physical world has seven wonders. The Internet has quite a few more wonders than seven. Text, images, and audio all abound online in different places and formats in an effort to directly engage with the human experience. Video games have created visceral experiences unlike anything a person could practically do in their physical existence. Furthermore, software-based simulations have taken unique pursuits like flying a plane, managing sports teams, living as a goat, city planning, motorsports, and farming, and they have turned these activities into enjoyable games.

Virtual reality (VR) is making digital endeavors even more visceral by placing high-quality lenses in front of a user's eyes, which stare into small, yet often higher than 2k in quality, miniature monitors. The best quality headsets almost entirely take up someone's vision, allowing them to be visually immersed in a world. More often than not, simulation games are still in the form of traditional flat-screen games, but VR is rapidly improving, and systems like the Valve Index have controllers that strap to a person's hands and can detect where their fingers are located, the position of their arms, and the headset tracks the motion of their head. Running a VR system like the Index requires slightly more computational grunt than a standard PC, and its minimum system requirements are 8 GB of RAM, an Nvidia GeForce GTX 970 or an AMD RX 480 GPU, accompanied by a "Dual Core with Hyper-Threading" CPU, as per Valve's website. In terms of computers built for gaming, these components are mainstays of the average setup.

The videogame VRChat is one of the more unique games to be experienced and an interesting place to visit online. VRChat tends to feel more like a weird and trippy bar than a video game. VRChat, as the name implies, is a virtual reality game, and it is optimally played with a VR headset such as a Valve Index or Oculus, but many other VR devices are supported. Players also have the option to play the game with a standard monitor, referred to as a flatscreen.

When in-game in VRChat, the player can move their head and arms around, and subsequently, their headset and controllers will move, which the game uses to control the player's character. Characters can be downloaded from a huge catalog of user creations, and they can also be made completely from scratch. Additionally, there are games within VRChat that the player can enjoy, such as billiards, capture the flag, and various first-person shooters. Naturally, the game intends chatting to be a mainstay of the title's experience. Many game modes have been created by the community, and the overarching theme of VRChat is that its success thrives from its community, which creates most of the experiences the game delivers to its player base. That same player base is the supplier of conversations for which the game is well known. Numerous different lobbies are in VRChat that a player can visit to simply chat or play a game together. Players can speak to one another via proximity chat while in a lobby.

For years, the idea of a virtual reality setting where anyone could enter a digital world and virtually engage together as if they were in person has existed, and VRChat has stepped closer to achieving that concept. However, surrealism is more prevalent in caricatures (such as a litany of anime models) and settings than photo-real graphics, which attempt to replicate two people's interactions 1:1.

Altogether, VRChat is a thoroughly weird experience, and that is pretty much par for the course, considering it is a game centered around various virtual reality settings where people want to see interesting visuals, but this game is also very unique in an uncanny and odd way. VR games are getting more visually elaborate and tactilely advanced with their controllers; they currently look incredible, and the interactions in the world feel very realistic. Using a VR headset truly looks like everything around the user is plausibly real, but of course, there are no sensations to feel, like a breeze or heat from the sun or that type of everyday realism. The fact remains that gaming is not far away from developing a technology that closely imitates reality, and in the next decade, progress in this realm will allow for a nearly replicated in-person experience.

Many people state that they enjoy VRChat and VR games as a whole because they are an escape from reality (see Steam reviews). These types of games are an incredible experience that more people should try, but there is certainly some concern for the welfare of the people who extensively engage with VR games. Escapist ideologies are important to lean on for relaxation occasionally, but at what point is recreating your own reality unhealthy? As mentioned before, VRChat is a weird place full of atypical people, but it is not too dissimilar from today's society.

The Web is bringing about all kinds of changes in communication. The number of people it is possible to meet online is quite overwhelming, and the shallow and ungratifying contact can leave many people feeling distraught. Many public figures complain about the negative attention they sometimes receive, and it must certainly be extremely uncomfortable to receive thousands of hateful messages due to some fairly insignificant incident. Due to the veil between a person and the online world, people do not tend to hold any punches when criticizing someone, and anyone who has spent time on YouTube or Twitter has witnessed longwinded cursing, temper tantrums, and threats of harm by users hiding behind the shield of anonymity the Internet provides. Communication online sometimes resembles road rage; when driving on the road, people only see a thing (car) and not a person. This effect seems to enhance people's more negative social interactions.

· · · ·

We are going to go on a digital adventure. The purpose of the Internet, outlined in previous chapters and described by Berners-Lee, is to be a semantic entity. Semantics, in this case, is a collection of things knitted together to create one thing, and that sounds quite a lot like what the Internet is.

The connections between not just webpages but the concepts those pages contain are important in understanding how search engines function, how people learn, and how the Web can be improved. These three concepts are all totally intertwined.

The adventure we are going to go on will be an attempt to explore how closely two completely different things are related. In the real world, giraffes and technology are definitely not closely related. Giraffes are not known to use technology (at least not to my knowledge), and technology has almost no focus on involving giraffes in the scientific progress of humanity. Both these truths are obvious. However, we are going to objectively figure out how these two random things are connected or at least how the Internet has made semantic connections between them.

The landscape of our adventure is (not surprisingly) the Web, and we will begin searching from a random page on the technology-focused news website *The Verge*. I chose *The Verge* because I believe this site should be positioned super far from anything to do with giraffes –a reasonable guess, or so I assume. Our adventure will conclude when we finish navigating to the *Wikipedia* page for giraffes. *Wikipedia* is heavily hyperlinked (a simple example of semantics in code), and this should make it fairly straightforward to navigate to the giraffe page once we arrive at a random *Wikipedia* page.

The technique I will use to click links is vital to the game we are going to play. I am going to borrow the term 'hop' from networking to describe how we will travel from site to site, and these hops will be counted to quantify how similar a roughly random news site is to a roughly random webpage about giraffes, although my ability to navigate will have an effect on this as I will have to be a human search engine. I am not sure how well that will go; hopefully not, but this may take nearly fifty hops if I were to hazard a guess.

To begin our adventure, I have chosen to start on *The Verge*'s page for the article "Plugged in and logged on: A History of the Internet on Film and TV" by Alexis Ong, which was chosen simply because it has 'Internet' in the title and was unlikely to contain anything about giraffes, which is our lofty end goal. A critical rule of this game is that I can only click on links; that way, I will hop from site to site only by direct connections, which are the embedded hyperlinks. During this adventure, I will hover over hyperlinked words to see where they go to help avoid going to dead ends. This is the part where I will act somewhat like a human search engine. Webpages tend to have a footer at the bottom of the page that contains various legalese and contact information. I think that these footers may be a helpful tool in navigating to our end destination on the giraffe *Wikipedia* page.

I am looking through the starting article and hovering over hyperlinked words to try and find something that appears to be inching closer to *Wikipedia*. Once we arrive at *Wikipedia*, I doubt it will take much more than a dozen hops to get to the page on giraffes. However, actually getting to *Wikipedia* may be quite difficult. Navigating through different websites can lead to some simplistic sites that have very few links to other pages, which is essentially a Web pitfall on our journey. I am looking to avoid these dead ends, and I will continue searching for website links that I believe will have numerous hyperlinks on them so we can better select the next hops.

<u>Starting page, "Plugged in and logged on: a history of the Internet on film and TV" published by *The Verge* and written by Alexis Ong</u>

Looking through the starting page's hyperlinks is not immediately encouraging. One of the links I clicked returned a 404 era. The Web is ever-changing, and sometimes pages are moved or removed. After hovering over several hyperlinks with my mouse cursor and viewing their destination at the bottom right of my Firefox browser, we have found some rather good fortune. While referencing the film *Sneakers,* the writer Ong cites "phreaking" as a concept from that film, and as luck would have it, the word is hyperlinked to phreaking's *Wikipedia* page.

<u>First Hop, *Wikipedia*: Phreaking</u>

Phreaking generally deals with hacking and experimenting with telephone systems. To give an example, when telephones became a common consumer utility, phreaks (as they are called) would sometimes use whistles to imitate dial tones to trick the phone system and do things like make free phone calls. Phreaking was one of the first instances of hacking in a networking adjacent field and illicitly manipulating technology as a whole.

Fortunately, we are only on our second hop, and we have already arrived at one of the most heavily semantic websites I know of. We are on *Wikipedia*. My strategy is now to look through the different links on this page and see if I can find something loosely related to animals or other things that might be in the obscure realm of giraffes. Not surprisingly, phreaking's page contains nothing about animals, but it is a fairly long article, so we do have a decent selection of where to hop next.

<u>Second Hop, *Wikipedia*: Internet</u>

I have concluded there is nothing too tangibly similar to giraffes on phreaking's page. What a crying shame. So, I believe we should next go to the Internet's *Wikipedia* article. The Internet's article is huge, and it has an extensive number of links to *Wikipedia* and other websites. I am searching through the page to see if I can find anything about animals.

On the Internet's page, there is a section about zero-rating, which is Internet access that is free with some minor stipulations such as having advertisements, the article explains. One of the nations mentioned that has this type of service is Kenya. I am not positive, but I think there are giraffes in Kenya.

<u>Third Hop, *Wikipedia*: Kenya</u>

We have rapidly departed from a news website to a completely different section of the Web. Many *Wikipedia* pages about countries have a section about wildlife that is local to the place. Hopefully, this page will contain some information about giraffes.

After a brief ctrl + f word search, this page contains no mention of the word giraffe. However, I did see a picture embedded into the page of elephants walking in a line. I am no animal expert, but when I see elephants, surely there must be some giraffes nearby. Kenya's *Wikipedia* page does have a section on wilderness areas.

<u>Fourth Hop, *Wikipedia*: Amboseli National Park</u>

This is a wildlife park in Kenya. Scrolling down to the page's "Wildlife" section, there is a hyperlink on a couple of attached words: Masai giraffe. It turns out there are giraffes in Kenya. We are certainly in luck, and we must be quite close to our final destination.

<u>Fifth Hop, *Wikipedia*: Masai giraffe</u>

The first paragraph on this page discusses giraffes and their species. Giraffes are described as the overarching genus, and there is, of course, a link to the word more general species of giraffe on this *Wikipedia* page.

<u>Sixth Hop, *Wikipedia*: Giraffe</u>

I am quite surprised that it only took six hops to go from an article about the Internet in media to a lengthy description all about giraffes.

•••

My initial guess that it would take fifty clicks to hop from *The Verge* to *Wikipedia*'s giraffe page was nowhere near accurate. I think that we were lucky that the news article contained a link to *Wikipedia*. I would not have bet on that. After all, *Wikipedia* is a great resource, especially considering many subjects do not have an outlet where writers have taken the time to research and explain a subject; in that case, *Wikipedia* creates a platform that can be expanded upon and improved over time. Finding the phreaking article (I do not mean to curse) was dumb luck, but it does go to show, firstly, that random webpages can contain scores or even hundreds of links, and secondly, the Internet is all fairly closely intertwined. I knew that once we arrived on *Wikipedia*, the related information would be fairly easy to find. This is a great showcase of the mechanics of semantics on the World Wide Web. Furthermore, this demonstration shows how important it is to build a website that properly links references so that search engines and people can find it. News articles are especially pertinent to this guidance because they are the modern way of referencing concepts both for validation and for the betterment of information sharing.

· · · ·

What a peculiar game to play; I am pretty sure we won. After all, we did make it to the end; it was only the briefness of the journey that surprised me. With the Internet, it is hard to lose when playing a game, but it is easy to get lost.

Ontologies are a result of semantics, which is a heavily syllabic way of saying everything is related, and for the above examples, we have shown the relations step by step. Experiments of thought are difficult to conclude upon, but it is reassuring to know the Web is held together so neatly, while it is a shame to think other connections like advertisements are completely shackling and rob people of their own decision-making when they replace more honest and informative pages.

Collective digital interconnectedness was far too long of a phrase to name the network of networks; the Internet had to suffice. But thankfully, there are a few good tests you or I can still explore to prove how useful the Web can be to a person. Things are like other things, at least in some ways, and that is the essence of the Internet. Everything is related to the simple parts of packet switching, eventually consisting of binary bits being sent on a wire.

Chapter 13 – Avoiding Network Blocks

Navigating through government-created restrictions or restrictions put in place by other organizations is often not too difficult. Technologically savvy governments are able to acquire information from companies that store data to track people's activities online, which can closely relate to what they do in their daily lives. Emails are quite an easy thing for law enforcement and hackers to acquire, whether they should be legally able to or not. From an individual's perspective, skirting censorship is easy, but remaining anonymous while doing so is not. The reason that advertisements relate to emails in an inbox is that email providers evaluate emails, and that data is often shared with other companies. Encrypted email is one of the best ways to securely communicate using Tor because almost no security exists for a traditional email inbox.

A VPN is a virtual private network. A VPN works by connecting a device over the Internet to a network that contains the VPN, and then the original traffic is routed through the VPN, enabling traffic to appear to be originating from a different hop. One of the simplest uses of a VPN is to hide the originating IP of a device. VPNs also use encryption to help mask any identifiable attributes of the devices that access their server. For example, if a user was in Germany but wanted to connect to a French website, which happened to block all non-French traffic, they could connect to a VPN in France so their packet header shows the website the traffic originates from France. In some cases, servers receiving the packets over the Internet are still able to analyze where the initial IP connection comes from and then proceed to block the traffic. The connection to a VPN is called a virtual private connection. Geo-blocking is when a firewall restricts IPs from certain regions from passing through. Certain nations, such as China, have national firewalls that prevent people inside the country from accessing certain sites. Alternatively, many nations geo-block traffic from countries that are known to frequently have illicit traffic or spread malware. VPNs have become very important in allowing Internet users to navigate around restrictions and censorship that are accomplished by geo-blocking, which may be both inbound and outbound.

Using VPNs often coincides with avoiding geo-blocking from firewalls. Website server hosts may have more restrictions than any outgoing part of a connection handshake. Websites commonly block access to their site from certain nations, and public IP addresses are always affiliated with a city and nation. For regular consumer use, traffic is frequently blocked because of differences in media trademarks in different geographical regions. The streaming service Netflix is not accessible from all countries because the videos they digitally deliver have intellectual property ownership in different places. Red tape for such issues is usually removed with the standard type of VPN, although in some cases, this type of connection will not completely hide a user's original IP, and many sites will block the VPN if they know the range of subnets the service uses. Site-to-site VPNs are used for the most secure connections and describe a route that only uses internal connections; these types of VPCs do not use the public Internet, unlike consumer VPNs.

In general, paid VPNs are more effective than free-to-use VPNs. Free VPNs are typically supported by ads and are usually much slower when browsing.

To explain the specifics of how a VPN functions, firewall rules should first be outlined. Blocking a website consists of blocking its domain name. For example, to block the Internet Archive, a firewall administrator would block the domain name archive.org. However, that is not all that needs to be done to block a site. Although that would work to block a site if the DNS (Domain Name System) server displays its name, using the site's IP could garner access to the site. So, to block a website more effectively, both its domain and IP range need to be blocked. The problem with blocking a range of IPs is that sites can use different IPs in different locations for load balancing, which is one way of avoiding censorship. Knowing what is blocked needs to be understood by both organizations preventing access to parts of the Internet and people avoiding censorship, and thus, an arm's race exists between these two parties.

Proxy servers are a more general device that alters how traffic passes through the server. Several different types of proxy servers exist, but in general, they act as an intermediary hop before a computer can connect to the Internet. Browsers can use extensions to obfuscate traffic to the Internet, but they only do so for tasks completed in the browser, not the entire device, which does not do much to hide activity on devices like smartphones that commonly use apps that connect to the Internet. In this way, proxies are similar to a VPN, but VPNs have their connections encrypted. Proxies are also used to regulate network traffic using load balancing when there is a significant influx of traffic.

Chapter 14 – Searching for the Lost

P eople look to the Internet to search for all kinds of things. One of the most critical and time-sensitive is the search for missing persons, especially those who have been kidnapped or are victims of human trafficking. Traditional methods of searching for these lost people, such as hanging up posters and walking around the community, are extremely time-consuming and do not always produce effective results. Investigative services, both police and private, have had substantial success in using social media to discover a person's whereabouts. Even when a lost person may not be able to contact the police, they likely know someone who is at least somewhat familiar with where they may be, although that person might not know they are considered missing. Things become complicated when trying to contact those acquaintances with the lost person because the acquaintance may also have no idea the person is lost. Understanding social connections is extremely important because the Internet has made social interactions far broader, and geolocation no longer matters in terms of who a person knows and has formed relationships with. Online friends may be able to help when tracking down a culprit (who does not want to be found) needs to be done quickly and with the most effective results. Generally, the way people are tracked online is an invasion of privacy, but it can certainly help find a person when they have been kidnapped.

A technology available from both Google and Bing is reverse image searching. Reverse image searching is when an image is either uploaded or a link is provided to the image, and the search engine then uses computer vision algorithms to find similar images. AI strategies like CV can greatly help in finding images of people using a search engine, assuming new pictures are being taken of a lost person, or if they accidentally appear online by coincidence. CV strategies are rapidly improving, and because of social media, many people have several pictures of themselves online, which can be used to help find them if they are lost. The more media, the better because some images are easier for CV to evaluate the image due to quality, lighting, or other factors that degrade image fidelity.

Photos taken by many types of phones and cameras have substantial metadata attached to the photo. One of the initial purposes of this metadata was to describe what kind of camera settings were used to take a photo, such as color settings and shutter speed. Sometimes, a piece of the metadata is the geographic coordinates where the photo was snapped. Most people do not realize how much information they might be giving away when they post a photo online, especially when it was taken with a device that, by default, attaches a substantial amount of metadata to a photo. Jimpl is one example of a website that evaluates metadata for an uploaded image, and there are many others like it that are just as easy to use.

• • • •

In the United States, there is an organization called NamUS (National Missing and Unidentified Persons System). The mission of NamUS is to resolve cases that are relevant to missing persons and identify human remains. Social media and search engine websites cache data about their users. These cookies maintain data on a user to help improve the user's experience while on the website. However, there are other ways people are tracked on the Internet that are more pertinent to providing evidence for someone's location. According to NamUS in their January 2024 Bi-Annual Report, there are roughly 23,972 missing persons in the United States and its territories. Nearly 600,000 people are reported missing every year. When an individual goes missing, usually their family or friends file a report with the police to assist in searching for them. Most missing persons are eventually found.

The Internet is one of the best places to start when searching for a missing person. Several organizations work to help recover people who have been lost. Individuals use Google for an extremely broad range of reasons, but today, users seek search engines to help find individuals who are frequently in danger.

Open-source intelligence (OSINT) is widely available on the Internet. In matters of national security, federal organizations rely on OSINT to gain information about certain things. An extremely important use of OSINT is in the search for persons who are missing. Social media sites, forums, and other publicly accessible places online can help searchers find people who may be in grave danger, such as those who are victims of human trafficking. Although some sources of this type of intelligence are readily available, others are more difficult to attain, which is an area where some white hat hackers may provide assistance. One example of this is hacking into a missing person's social media account to gain a better understanding of when their activity was and potentially from what locations. Much of that information is visible on their public posts, but having access to their devices and accounts would elaborate further on their past communications with people and their activities, which may have led to their disappearance.

The problem with finding someone is not always that there is minimal information about them; there may be too much. This type of information flood is common when dealing with Internet-adjacent entities, like people. People who are very active online have a huge cache of information about themselves located around the Web. Finding all the relevant information on a missing person is the most difficult thing to attain. NamUS helps people engage with law enforcement and other organizations that use OSINT, as well as more private information, to help build a case for discovering someone's whereabouts and other more unfortunate situations that determine the identity of a person's remains.

Any individual can begin a search for a person by entering data relevant to the missing person's physical attributes and appearance, last known location, and circumstances surrounding their disappearance.

The World Wide Web has caused information to create rings around Internet users. These rings often overlap with their family, friends, coworkers, neighbors, and other acquaintances. The social relationships that exist via the Internet are unusual and frequently stem from a common interest, but most people online are well acquainted with people they have never physically met. Gaming communities, professional online work relationships, social network interactions with family, and other Web interactions are all a part of the network missing persons can be affiliated with. These outer social rings may also exist on social websites with numerous users or even large online communities and can greatly help in finding people, specifically minors, who engage with gaming-focused communities such as Discord and gaming platforms like Steam.

Being able to directly access someone's smartphone or computer would help tremendously in understanding their activities. It would be simple to view not only their browsing data but also their past email communications by evaluating cached data with forensic analysis software like Autopsy, which can run on Linux, MacOS, and Windows. The company ADF Solutions also makes USB products that scan Android and MacOS smartphones for forensic data. Application usage and changes can be seen in the Event Viewer of all Windows machines on the physical side of the situation while accessing a user's account inside the application would be the best way to view their activity for social apps. If someone spends a few hours a day on a computer, evaluating their device will definitely provide elaborate details about their recent behavior.

. . . .

The New York City Police Department (NYPD) has taken action since 2014 to increase its presence on Twitter. The NYPD is the largest police department in the United States. Much of their efforts to increase visibility on social media has been to help engage and share information with the public about missing persons. One of the most common ways to find a missing person, especially if their presumed location is limited to a city or county, is to hang up posters with an image of the missing person. However, not everyone walking by these posters is going to intently analyze these images, probably because they presume that they do not know anything about the missing individual. This is why the Internet is vital in recovering people who have been reported missing. NYPD has posted images and videos on their social media sites to help show people images of missing children to people who are more interested in helping and potentially more knowledgeable about a person's whereabouts. The purpose of amber alerts is to use the Wireless Emergency Alerts (WEA) system to immediately begin a location-based search for a child. However, amber alerts are not very effective when they are slowly released, assuming the persons involved are in transit.

The way people use their devices and engage with the Web causes much of their activity to be stored somewhere. Accessing this valuable information can significantly help in the quest for recovering people who need help. Hacking and device forensics are as pertinent as ever in understanding people's habits.

Chapter 15 – Looking to the Future

Capturing the essence of the Internet is not an easy task. Some of its most important contents are being lost, and the online world has had important influences on culture that are being forgotten. The nature of technology is that it is changing for the sake of improvement all the time. Not only is the information available online increasing, but the websites and services that are available are also constantly rotating in and out, becoming new while others are abandoned, such as MySpace and its well-known rise and fall in popularity. Certainly, many more social sites will come and go in the next few years as they become overtaken by more popular alternatives. Social networking trends are critically important in understanding how people of the world engage with each other when there are no borders, no physical barriers, and fewer social repercussions.

Websites online are a very stagnant target. The HTML of individual pages can be easily viewed, which allows Web developers to borrow content from sites (pressing F12 while on a webpage brings up the code the page was written with). Because of this partial open-source availability of code, it is not difficult for large tech companies to one-up the competition and make improvements on a concept. However, this concept does leave many people wondering why developers neglect to make websites better geared for specific devices such as desktop computers and smartphones, which have drastically different-sized screens, leading to bad viewing experiences when that is not accounted for. Some websites act like most people engage with their content on a PC, whereas smartphone use is much more popular than a traditional desktop or laptop computer in this day and age. Viewing a properly scaled website on a smartphone is a real rarity.

The online storefront eBay has been around since 1995, and since then, it has garnered several competitors. Taobao is an online marketplace similar to eBay, where users buy and sell things. Taobao is owned by Alibaba and is headquartered in Hangzhou, China. Much of Taobao is based on eBay, but since its inception in 2003, the companies have changed slightly in their respective development roadmaps, some of which are to better fulfill their regional markets' wants, especially since Taobao only operates in Chinese-speaking regions which traditionally follow different storefront styles and website layouts. Naturally, some of the similarities in these two companies also result from differing laws that concern copyright infringement.

Similar competition exists all over the Internet; a company maintains a website, and competitors vie for clicks and attention for their site. The Web thrives on innovation and constantly improving, or at least trying to improve, in an ever-changing landscape online. Consumers can access and buy products from sites they are visiting for the very first time in a matter of a couple of minutes, and although some familiarity is beneficial, customers tend not to have much loyalty to where they shop online, especially if a positive browsing experience entices them to use a new marketplace. Although copyright laws are not always respected in China, open-source resources enhance numerous websites' APIs. Various open-source programs are on GitHub that allow anyone with the know-how to use and manipulate their code for whatever purpose they choose. The community development aspects of the Internet are great for innovation, although simultaneously, large companies can be easily outpaced and grow stagnant when they fail to deliver products and services that create a palpable improvement. The movement of open-source has enabled many startups to thrive in making free software, not to mention the litany of tech companies that have been around for less than ten years, many of which rely on things like Apache servers for open-source enterprise solutions. On the software side of things, projects like Linux, VLC media player, the image editing software GIMP, and the prolific 7-Zip are all free open-source projects that billions of people have used.

Once the Web became a place that much of the general public was able to access, the concept of Web 1.0 was born, although that expression is used mostly in retrospect and was not very common during that era. Starting in 2004, the era of Web 2.0 began, and that era continues today. However, a new concept has been edging nearer to existence in recent years. Web 3.0 was initially conceived by Berners-Lee and supported by the World Wide Web Consortium (W3C), a group that supplies standards for the Web in the name of improvement and standard use across numerous platforms. Berners-Lee coined the term Semantic Web, which describes how he wanted webpages to become machine-readable, helping with easier indexing and navigation. The most straightforward example of this integration into pages has to do with how the code of a webpage is written to help hyperlink content to similar concepts; at least, that is how a human would navigate. For machine-readable sites, it is indexed differently than that.

The clunky name Resource Description Framework in Attributes (RDFa) is what these types of attributes are called in code, and they essentially add a coded link to the HTML that is the backend of the page. To exemplify this standard, on *Wikipedia*, viewing the page for "Car" shows numerous hyperlinks such as for "motor vehicle" and "wheels." RDFa's purpose is to more seamlessly attach similar webpages together, which, on a website of articles like *Wikipedia*, is organized and quite easy to do. When reading through the same page on cars, clicking on "Ford Model T" (one of the first cars in production), a reader can quickly navigate to other related manufacturers and even find links outside of *Wikipedia* to official company websites. A huge benefit of this standardization is it greatly helps people find similar things to what they are looking for, which is a powerful tool considering people learn by assimilating new knowledge into what they previously know, or in this example, what they first look up online. Furthermore, machines are also much more capable of navigating through these links and forming webbed connections from common terms to more obscure concepts.

Web 3.0 (the Semantic Web) should not be confused with Web3, which refers to a more decentralized economy that results from Internet use and how it has increased the breadth of the market by ignoring national borders. The term Web3 is used in marketing jargon and has little practical purpose.

"The Semantic Web" was an essay that introduced the self-titled concept that encourages standards among Web-based content, especially catering to information being more readily used by machines. The essay further elaborates on how this will establish connections in a person's life and better organize daily events. The term "agents" is frequently used by Berners-Lee in his, James Hendler, and Ora Lassila's description of how a modern Web should continue to be developed for synchronicity. Despite the capabilities of AI systems today, Web semantics were contrived well before machine learning had widespread use cases. However, webpages structured for the purpose of supporting a Semantic Web would ultimately assist AI in sorting through information, more specifically in the context of search engines, which heavily benefit from clear yet detailed HTML code. Of course, the reason for this foundational reasoning is to fix the problem from the core (code) rather than using the brute-force power of machine learning algorithms to sort through massive data pools.

· · · ·

Most laws are nationalized when it comes to the online legislature, and some regional governments, like the European Union, also have more broadly enforced laws. That is all well and good, but rules are only pertinent to websites hosted in those countries. Meanwhile, users in regulated countries are free to connect to any website they choose, assuming they are not restricted by government firewalls. The Internet does not and should not belong to anyone. The Internet cannot be easily controlled, and it is fair to say that most legislation intended to control Internet traffic is useless and sometimes silly in how ill-suited it is, and free people and those who are proponents of freely distributed information are thankful for this fact. In terms of Internet and information accessibility, there will always be more loopholes than there are means of preventing access to resources online.

A practical example of this is that in the fictional nation of The Nineland Confederation, the fictional and obscure drug ralphihol is illegal. However, on the border of Nineland is the fictionally proud nation of The Toxicate Republic. Ralphihol is not regulated in any way in Toxicate. If a proud and free-thinking citizen of Nineland wished to connect to a website that sold ralphihol and was hosted in Toxicate, normally, nothing would stop them. Going further, the individual orders an unspecified quantity of the fairly potent ralphihol from Toxicate, who, as mentioned, does not have any laws concerning ralphihol. The buyer's order is completed, and they receive their illicit goods, and capitalism prospers for yet another day to the chagrin of Nineland's ineffective legislature.

Freedom exists on the Web. No other places seem to enable such a radical idea. Maybe it has become too cliché to let people live without organizations demanding their complacency.

Certain domains have systems configured to intercept traffic to the site before it arrives. This type of intermediary server protects the end site and disrupts DDoS (distributed denial of service) attacks while also helping to prevent an overwhelming amount of non-malicious traffic from causing an outage.

Normally, the simplest way to achieve a similar effect would be to use a VPN to dodge geo-blocking, but webmasters can take steps to allow anyone to access their sites better, regardless of where they are. A common way to achieve this is to have the same websites but with different servers located in different regions for better accessibility.

• • • •

The Web's progression has no specific trajectory. However, the commercialization of the Web has contributed greatly to a worse experience for all people participating in interactions online. Escaping from consumer targeting online is nigh impossible, and to be born anew online is nearly unreachable because applications and websites will continue to track all of their user's IPs, which is unfortunately always handed over to the server when the metaphorical Web discussion begins. Web 2.0 is noted as being an era of significant corporate control; Web 3.0 is an ambitious goal for less overreach.

Chapter 16 – Privacy

Digital privacy has become a major concern for consumers and businesses as personal information becomes more abundant online. Issues have been brought to light regarding how companies use and sell information that they have harvested from their customers or other people who have been in contact with their Web servers. Being anonymous online is nearly impossible, and companies frequently fail to protect customer data when data breaches occur or when the business itself is participating in dishonest practices, such as failing to inform patrons about how they are using their data. Although this statement may seem sweeping, the fact remains true that much of what everyone does online is being tracked by way of cached data. This chapter will outline not only how privacy is compromised but also how individuals can protect themselves online from digital encroachment and outright theft of information.

The information security expert Roger Clarke published a paper in 1988 titled "Information Technology and Dataveillance." Clarke was the first to introduce the term dataveillance in his essay, which was rather timely considering Berners-Lee first conceptualized the World Wide Web in 1989, and subsequently, the Web went public in 1991 and further increased in size due to the general public creating websites in the early 1990s. Clarke's essay recognized and explained how information systems would become configured to collect and use individuals' data. However, Clarke's narrative remains fairly neutral, and some more positive aspects of dataveillance, like trends from large data pools, are detailed. Theories are not harmful to anyone, but palpable mechanisms certainly can be. As AI training becomes more common (especially on search engines), individuals need to pay attention to how their data is ingested, even if they are only a drop in the pool.

• • • •

A critical cybersecurity principle of protecting assets that are exposed to the Internet in any way is setting a good quality passphrase. This piece of advice is well known among anyone remotely competent in security, but it is rarely implemented among employees or individuals due to one factor: lack of creativity. Remembering a twelve-character (or more) passphrase is difficult. Ironically, good passwords do not contain words or phrases; they are randomized gibberish. The most difficult-to-crack password/passphrase hashes are generated from an application and not by hand. KeePass is an example of an easy-to-use desktop application that manages passwords, although there are many others that are similar. Android and iOS also have numerous password managers from which to choose. Password managers function by having a master password unlock the application, granting access to usernames and passwords that can be copied and pasted. KeePass also has the ability to require a designated file, such as a picture, to be on a device before it can unlock and use its database, preventing someone who knows the database password from gaining access.

Password managers generate passwords based on cracking strength, which is measured in bits. More bits equate to a stronger password. Twelve characters is a decent minimum for password length. However, the strength of the password hash is effectively measured by the characters used. The password "fantastic133" will have a much weaker hash to be cracked than "*2ZhNA^$x749," a much more randomized password, although they are the same character length.

The big three Web browsers do, of course, store passwords but in a manner that is completely insecure. Browsers store encrypted passwords in a folder. The passwords are, indeed, encrypted, but the encryption key can be found on the same device. Web browser developers could have gone about setting up their security for stored passwords in a different way, but this flimsy (like a hammock made of dental floss) development decision makes Web browser password storage a bad security choice.

Hashcat (technically oclHashcat) is a utility that de-hashes passwords. Other utilities exist for de-hashing, all of which function with the help of graphics processing units. It may seem odd that a GPU is super effective at hashing functions because it has nothing to do with 'graphics,' but the structure of a GPU's cores is different than a CPU (Central Processing Unit), and the way GPU memory is allocated is also better suited for hashing tasks. When using randomly generated passwords, there is less likelihood of the password appearing on the huge lists of passwords hackers use to log into accounts, which is usually easier than using a GPU to discover the password's hash. Master lists like these are compiled from breaches.

• • • •

The most important part of how a website recognizes and maintains information on a user is with cookies. Privacy and cookies go hand in hand. Anyone who has ever visited a website has probably been asked by the site if they would give permission to store cookies. A web browser stores the cookies locally and gives these metadata files to the site when connecting. The reason an account is still logged in when returning to a site is because of authentication cookies. Most of the catered features a website delivers to a certain user are stored in cookies. In countries within the European Union, it is law to state that a website uses cookies for nonessential purposes.

Louis J. Montulli II, a well-known programmer who developed Web browsers in the early 1990s, coined the term cookies to describe these small but crucial pieces of data. While working for Netscape, Montulli desired to create a way for servers to remember their visitors and improve their experience. Initial attempts at solving this problem were difficult for Montulli and his team because he knew that creating a way that ultimately tracked a user was an invasion of privacy, and that was certainly now what he wished to accomplish. One of the first uses of cookies was to maintain a virtual shopping cart after a visitor had left a website, which is still around today.

Session cookies are deleted after a website visitor leaves, while persistent cookies, which are the most controversial type of data shared (often inadvertently) with a Web server, continue to be stored on a browser. Websites receive these types of cookies whenever a user reconnects to a site and tracks when they reconnect. Having access to a device's cookies helps show what a user browses, and that results in businesses targeting them with advertisements for related products.

Third-party cookies are the most controversial cookies because they are used on websites frequently without their visitor's consent. Digital ad companies have their own algorithms and methods for serving ads that they believe people will click on based on their past activity. The images that accompany advertisements cause cookies to be stored on the visitor's computer, and ad companies like Alphabet, Meta, Microsoft, and Alibaba track what advertisements people click on. Unfortunately, the barrage of ads on the Web is quietly preventing people from controlling their own experiences when browsing the Internet. Instead, corporations are making decisions about what ads they see, and in the case of many of these platforms, that also affects the kinds of posts and content they are displayed in social media because these ad companies and social media platforms are one and the same.

Chapter 17 – Digital Underground

The dark web is a mysterious and frequently illicit collection of domains on the Internet. Interestingly, the dark web's contents are considerably vast, making up about 5-10% of the Internet's total size.

Distinguishing between the dark web and the clear Web (otherwise known as the regular World Wide Web or Clearnet) is relatively simple, and the variance consists of the difference in how a user browses through websites. Naturally, on the Clearnet, users use a Web browser to connect directly to domains. The major search engines display websites that are only on the clear Web and none that are dark websites.

Instead of using a Web browser like Chrome, Firefox, or Opera, individuals browse the dark web using the Tor browser. Tor stands for The Onion Router, which refers to how it routes packets through processes of layered encryption. Tor can be found at torproject.org. However, in countries with strict censorship, Tor's website is usually blocked. A simple way around this is to email the developers of Tor at gettor@torproject.org, and an automated email will send the necessary download files. For similar circumstances, Tor also has bridge connections that allow users to connect to Tor's network even when their ISP explicitly blocks traffic to Onion sites.

Dark Web traffic is encrypted differently than Clearnet traffic, and this encryption is what makes using the dark web special. HTTPS traffic is also encrypted on the Clearnet but with fewer layers than the routing techniques that the Tor browser (the dark web's standard browser) uses, hence its name. Rather than using normal top-level domains such as .com or .net, the Tor browser uses .onion to denote a website on the dark web. Furthermore, the dark web does not use typical domain names such as google.com; instead, most domains on the dark web would appear something like jxk3nc8.onion or other garbled nonsense in an attempt to keep the domain more anonymous. Dark Web domains frequently change, sometimes on a weekly or even daily basis, so they are more difficult to track, whereas that practice is rare on the Clearnet.

Several different marketplaces exist on the dark web, and frequently, these sites are shut down by various law enforcement agencies to only reappear days later as a rebranded place to buy goods, some of which are illicit. Drug marketplaces make up close to 15% of Onion services. Viewing drugs for sale on Onion sites is arguably less likely to result in physical danger than the traditional way of illicitly buying drugs, which, of course, is paying cash in person. This method of more accessible and anonymous transactions is why drug sales are so popular on the dark web. However, these illicit marketplaces are rife with fraudulent activity, and scammers abound in a market with almost no regulations. Most transactions on the dark web use the currency Bitcoin and Monero to pay for goods. Sometimes, stolen credit cards or stolen bank accounts are used to pay for things on various dark web marketplaces. Buying things on Onion sites is not inherently illegal, and there are plenty of legal transactions that can be made using electronic currencies for things like clothes or other items that are popularly sold on the Clearnet.

Onion routing was developed by the US Navy in the 1990s and patented in 1998. The most unique aspect of Onion encryption is the separation of its layers, which obfuscates where initial IP packets are sent from. The hops the packets make from router to router act like a sort of dead drop. For example, when an exchange takes place, a router located in the fictitious city of Placeville sends its packets to the next location, which is a router in Franktown. After the router in Franktown receives the communication, it is sent to a router in Location City. However, because of the layers of encryption, the device in Location City knows the packets came from Franktown (because its IP states as much) but has no way of knowing someone in Placeville, the initial sender, was the person who originated the communication. Additionally, none of the traversed locations know the contents of the data, which in some cases contains the actual evidence of illegal activity if the purpose of the dark web activity was to participate in something nefarious, although Tor's encryption can just as likely help to conceal an honest individual's identity. In this example, Placeville, Franktown, and Location City all contain volunteer servers that keep Tor's network up and running. Places like public libraries and universities are common hosts for Tor exit nodes. Since the dark web has a fraction of the servers that the standard Internet contains, connection speeds are typically not very fast.

Due to the anonymity granted (which is not always foolproof) by Onion browsing, individuals who are resisting being spied on also use these services. People such as whistleblowers often use Tor to communicate with media outlets to transfer information in a safer manner than direct communication, which can be more easily tracked when using the Clearnet and email. Being that Tor acts as a series of proxy servers, many Internet users living in nations that have strict censorship laws allow those people to access information and software to enhance their freedom to resist the censorship of nationalized firewalls. People fighting against domestic abuse and victims of stalking can also garner help from social workers by using Tor as a difficult-to-track means of communicating with organizations that can help these victims of abuse. Tor has a multitude of uses for better encryption and keeping user activity anonymous compared to the otherwise easily tracked Clearnet.

ProtonMail is one of the most popular services on the dark web. Using email on the dark web is important in shielding one's identity and is especially helpful in fighting against government censorship that hinders global communication. Using encrypted mail on the dark web also helps people anonymously provide tips to news outlets.

Different from either of the aforementioned groups of networks is the deep web, which consists of private websites that require specified access, such as with credentials, or may even block traffic that is not from specific IP addresses. The dark web is a small component of the larger deep web, but they are not exactly the same. Unindexed sites make up the deep web and systems involved with medical records, banking, members-only forums, and certain kinds of cloud storage. Deep web locations usually require connecting to the site using a specific Internet protocol or a company-specific VPN. Deep web pages cannot be searched for. With best practices in mind, these connections might vary by connection method (like a

Web browser or a company desktop application), but these systems are always accessed with a username, password, and some type of two-factor authentication, whether that be a phone app or a physical token like a YubiKey.

In professional networking services, firewalls are accessed and maintained on the deep web. Security engineers access these sites, usually by putting the device's IP and protocol into the Omnibox in a Web browser. The nature of all firewalls is that they face the Internet and shield the network behind it, so traffic is intercepted before entering a network DMZ (Demilitarized Zone). The amount of people who require access to a firewall is so small that IPs should be specifically permitted to connect to the firewall when needed, and such a configuration is made inside the firewall. All other traffic attempting to reach the firewall management site should effectively reach nothing, and they may receive an error when trying to visit the site on a browser to better conceal what the IP contains. The ease of use in being able to remotely manage a service like a firewall is helpful, but the security risk also needs to be weighed because anything connected to the Internet can be targeted by attackers.

$$\bullet\ \bullet\ \bullet\ \bullet$$

Another interesting aspect of the dark web is how it uses search engines. On the regular Web, it is not always easy to find websites. Much is the same on the dark web, except it is even more difficult because some sites are not interested in being easily found due to their main purpose being conducting what is considered to be a crime in many jurisdictions.

DuckDuckGo is a popular search engine that queries websites online on both the dark web and Clearnet. When using the Onion browser, DuckDuckGo is the default search engine. DuckDuckGo has always had principles of integrity since its inception, such as protecting the privacy of its users and not tracking their search activities. Even when searching Clearnet, DuckDuckGo does not produce the same results as traditional search engines. DuckDuckGo more commonly displays sites that may have been flagged (whether fairly or unfairly) by other popular search engines, causing them to never appear when searched for.

The contents of the dark web are peculiar and diverse. Sci-Hub is a library of scientific articles that can be downloaded and read without having to pay for the content. The computer programmer Alexandra Elbakyan founded Sci-Hub as a way to distribute scientific papers freely so that users can access scientific literature without paying the high costs of some of these publications. Furthermore, many scientific publications are difficult to find because their reader audience is tiny, and as papers get older, they only grow more obscure. However, many of these papers are copyrighted, and distributing them for free can be copyright infringement. With all these factors in mind (and some legalities ignored), Sci-Hub continues to operate for the betterment of education.

Browsing on the dark web can be hazardous. Using Tor is legal, but certain sites can contain content that is illegal to view. Additionally, there is nothing to regulate the dark web, so nothing stops websites from distributing malware to those visiting the site. To negate malware, dark web users might have a dedicated machine for dark web use that is frequently reimaged. Furthermore, using a virtual machine is the most practical way to browse the dark web.

• • • •

A fabled and infamous black market used to exist, which was very profitable and garnered significant media attention when it was temporarily shut down in 2013 by law enforcement and then closed for good in 2014. The platform was called Silk Road.

Ross William Ulbricht began the Silk Road in 2011. Ulbricht went by the handle Dread Pirate Roberts and managed the dark web marketplace along with other admins until it was shut down. The Silk Road existed as a virtual storefront and somewhat resembled Amazon's online store, with products being listed in rows and categories placed in a column along the left side. English was the language the site operated in (to give a vague idea of its clientele). An estimated 70% of the products sold on Silk Road were drugs, and much of the products still sold on the dark web today are pharmaceuticals. Drug sales were so prolific that they were listed by categories such as steroids, psychedelics, and stimulants on Silk Road. Unlike some dark web sites, Silk Road had a rule that items sold on the site could not "harm or defraud" people. This rule remained true and prevented illicit images involving children, weapons, hitman services, and stolen credit card numbers.

Not everything that was sold on Silk Road (and other sites on the dark web, for that matter) is illegal; there are many perfectly normal products for sale on the dark web, such as common consumer items you might see on a Clearnet site like eBay. Bitcoin was used to purchase goods on the Silk Road, and during court proceedings, it was revealed that Silk Road saw what is equivalent to $1.2 billion in transactions, earning the company $80 million worth of commissions. Despite the illegality of buying and selling drugs online and then additionally delivering the drugs through various mail systems, which is also highly illegal, there was such a significant demand that laws did not hinder transactions on the Silk Road or the dark web as a whole. However, US drug agencies had an undercover agent become an admin of the site, which helped to collect information on the dealings of the business, leading authorities to discover Dread Pirate Roberts's real identity. Later on, Ulbricht was arrested at the San Francisco Public Library location in Glen Park, where he was apprehended by the Federal Bureau of Investigation. A few months after that, Ulbricht was charged with narcotics conspiracy, engaging in a continuing criminal enterprise conspiracy to commit computer hacking, and money laundering, according to an FBI report. Ulbricht was sentenced to two life sentences without parole. He was also fined $183 million. Three other individuals were charged with crimes related to managing the Silk Road.

• • • •

If you were able to put part of the Internet into your pocket, if you were to chop off a piece of the world's media online, what would you choose to secure? Different people naturally have different dispositions for their favorite entertainment like movies, music, TV, games, and ebooks, but there exists a certain form that encapsulates these items of Internet entertainment and puts them on drives (or other portable storage devices) called El Paquette Semanal which translates from Cuban Spanish to English: The Weekly Package. This collection of media is one terabyte in size.

The Cuban government has numerous restrictions on what its residents can visit on the Internet, and the nation as a whole is significantly censored. Fortunately, more of Cuba is gaining Internet access, and about three-quarters of the country is able to go online. The masses will always want to commune with the network of networks even if they do not have a live connection to the Web, and that is why El Paquette Semanal was created. The collection of files features popular television shows, music, and films and is a good sample of what can be readily found online. The website for El Paquette can be found online at paquetesemanal.eltoque.com

Chapter 18 – A Note From the Author

I am not sure humanism is tasked to duel technology. Maybe it is more like a shepherd pressing digital sheep into the place they belong; perhaps that is the confrontation that needs resolving.

I am not sure if something is allowed to be perfect yet flawed, to be natural yet intrinsically dangerous. Perhaps that is what beauty is. The chaos of the Internet is what makes it so incredible; it is the digitization of society. We are approaching a point where people are so ingrained in online activities, like retrieving information and spending time with friends, that I feel I am unable to call the Internet the online world. There is no longer a recognizable difference between what is online and what is not, problems and all. Humans are far too social to stay out of the world's biggest digital discussion.

The first thing I ever published was *Artificial Intelligence in Short* because I knew there was a great need in literature for a concise, example-laden, and poignant book about AI that almost anyone somewhat proficient in technology could read and become equipped with a good knowledge of AI and its facets like computer vision. In *The State of The Internet: Living on the Network of Networks,* I really wanted to capture how unique the Web has become from a human perspective as well as how it is being manipulated by corporations. This sort of State of the Union seemed relevant because of how the Internet has changed in the last five years and how much it will continue to alter over the next five years.

Best wishes, and thank you for reading. I am on Goodreads; feel free to leave this book a rating or review there or anywhere you please. I am always writing amidst the genre of computers & technology as well as dark fantasy in my *Ossified Series*, where my second book will release in a few months.

References

C h1.
    none

Ch2.

Emtage, Alan. "Archie." In Intelligent information retrieval: The case of astronomy and related space sciences, pp. 103-111. Dordrecht: Springer Netherlands, 1993. https://link.springer.com/chapter/10.1007/978-0-585-33110-2_7

Gray, Matthew. "Credits and Background." Internet Growth and Statistics: Credits and Background, 1996. https://www.mit.edu/~mkgray/net/background.html.

Emerson Cook, Charles. "Pictures by Telegraph." Cook Pearson's Magazine, pp. 405. 1900. http://www.deadmedia.org/notes/27/279.html

Featherly, K."ARPANET." Encyclopedia Britannica, July 15, 2024. https://www.britannica.com/topic/ARPANET.

Fry, Stephen. "Stephenfry.com 2.0."Stephen Fry's Podgrams. Series 2 Episode 1. October, 2008. https://web.archive.org/web/20170404220105/http://www.podcasts.com/stephen_frys_podgrams_audio_visual/episode/series_2_episode_1_stephenfry.com_2.0

"The WWW Virtual Library." February, 2017. https://www.vlib.org/

Vetter, Ronald J., Chris Spell, and Charles Ward. "Mosaic and the world wide web." Computer 27, no. 10 (1994): 49-57. https://ieeexplore.ieee.org/abstract/document/318591

Hayes, Adam. "Dotcom Bubble Definition." Investopedia, May 21, 2024. https://www.investopedia.com/terms/d/dotcom-bubble.asp.

Ch.3

Weissman, Jonathan S. "The Time Is Still Now for IPv6." American Registry for Internet Numbers, May 18, 2022. https://www.arin.net/blog/2022/05/18/time-still-now-ipv6/.

Morr, Derek. "Verizon Mandates IPv6 Support for Next-Gen Cell Phones." CircleID Master, June 9, 2009. https://circleid.com/

"Mobile Network Coverage by Country, around the World." TheGlobalEconomy.com, 2016. https://www.theglobaleconomy.com/rankings/Mobile_network_coverage/.

Press, Gil. "How Many People Own Smartphones? (2024-2029)." What's The Big Data?, January 31, 2024. https://whatsthebigdata.com/smartphone-stats/.

"History of Commercial Radio." Federal Communications Commission, October 17, 2023. https://www.fcc.gov/media/radio/history-of-commercial-radio.

Ch. 4

Bush, Vannevar. "As We May Think." Atlantic Monthly, July (1945).

Schwartz, Barry. "How Google Uses Artificial Intelligence In Google Search." Search Engine Land, October 24, 2022. https://searchengineland.com/how-google-uses-artificial-intelligence-in-google-search-379746.

" In-Depth Guide to How Google Search Works." Google Search Central, April 22, 2024.

https://developers.google.com/search/docs/fundamentals/how-search-works.

Robison, Kylie. "Google Defends AI Search Results after They Told Us to Put Glue on Pizza." The Verge, May 31, 2024. https://www.theverge.com/2024/5/30/24168344/google-defends-ai-overviews-search-results.

Ch. 5

Lewis, Amanda Chicago. "The People Who Ruined the Internet." The Verge, November 1, 2023. https://www.theverge.com/features/23931789/seo-search-engine-optimization-experts-google-results.

Arthur, Charles. "Foundem Accuses Google of Using Its Power to Favour Own Links." The Guardian, November 30, 2010. https://www.theguardian.com/technology/2010/nov/30/google-foundem-ec-competition-rules.

Ch. 6

Ch. 7

Hawking, Stephen. "British Telecom Commercial by Stephen Hawking ." Who Sampled, 1994. https://www.whosampled.com/Stephen-Hawking/British-Telecom-Commercial/.

Pink Floyd – Keep Talking https://www.youtube.com/watch?v=wbOTkDn49qI

Project Gutenberg. Accessed August 27, 2024. https://www.gutenberg.org/.

Godin, Seth. "Can Ordinary People Become Leaders?" NPR, January 17, 2014. https://www.npr.org/transcripts/261096538.

Swartz, Jon. "Q&A with Stephen Hawking." USA Today, December 2, 2014. https://www.usatoday.com/story/tech/2014/12/02/stephen-hawking-intel-technology/18027597/.

Adams, Douglas. "Radio 4 in Four - 42 Douglas Adams Quotes to Live By." BBC Radio 4, 2024. https://www.bbc.co.uk/programmes/articles/2bcFfMt6rGLTPpbG0yLwPw0/42-douglas-adams-quotes-to-live-by.

Ch. 8

"Confidentiality, Integrity, and Availability: The CIA Triad." Office of Information Security, 2024. https://informationsecurity.wustl.edu/items/confidentiality-integrity-and-availability-the-cia-triad/.

Ch. 9

Insight NOKIA. "A History of the Copper Telephone Line." Nokia, August 6, 2014. https://www.nokia.com/blog/history-copper-telephone-line/.

Bastidas, Angel M. "World Boxing Association History." World Boxing Association, October 22, 2018. https://www.wbaboxing.com/wba-history/world-boxing-association-history.

Google Ngram Viewer: https://books.google.com/ngrams/graph?content=livestream&year_start=1800&year_end=2022&corpus=en&smoothing=3

Taylor, Frank. "Frankncats Twitch Channel." Twitch. Accessed August 28, 2024. https://www.twitch.tv/frankncats.

Popper, Ben. "Justin.Tv, the Live Video Pioneer That Birthed Twitch, Officially Shuts Down." The Verge, August 5, 2014. https://www.theverge.com/2014/8/5/5971939/justin-tv-the-live-video-pioneer-that-birthed-twitch-officially-shuts.

"Spotify Technology (SPOT) Market Cap & Net Worth." Stock Analysis. Accessed August 28, 2024. https://stockanalysis.com/

Ch. 10

Google Trends: https://trends.google.com/trending?geo=US&hours=168

Eser, Alexander. "Key Google Search Statistics Revealed: Impact and Insights Unveiled." Google Search Statistics Statistics: Market Data Report 2024, July 23, 2024. https://worldmetrics.org/google-search-statistics/.

Anderson, Porter. "US Publishers File Brief Opposing Internet Archive's Appeal." Publishing Perspectives, March 18, 2024. https://publishingperspectives.com/2024/03/us-publishers-file-a-brief-opposing-the-internet-archives-appeal/.

Ch. 11

Skinner, Burrhus F. "Reinforcement today." American Psychologist 13, no. 3 (1958): 94.

Ch. 12

"50 Years of Ebooks: 1971-2021." Project Gutenberg, 2021. https://www.gutenberg.org/about/background/50years.html.

"VALVE Index System Requirements." Steam Support. Accessed August 28, 2024. https://help.steampowered.com/en/faqs/view/105E-66E3-962A-1577.

Ch. 13

"The Difference between a VPN and a Web Proxy." Mozilla. Accessed August 28, 2024. https://www.mozilla.org/en-US/products/vpn/resource-center/the-difference-between-a-vpn-and-a-web-proxy/.

Ch. 14

Jimpl an "Online EXIF data viewer" https://jimpl.com/

"Reports & Statistics: Cases Created in NamUs June 2024
." NamUs, June 2024. https://namus.nij.ojp.gov/library/
reports-and-statistics.

"NYPD Newsroom." Newsroom - NYPD, 2024.
https://www.nyc.gov/site/nypd/media/newsroom/
newsroom-landing.page.

Ch. 15

Berners-Lee, Tim, James Hendler, and Ora Lassila. "The
Semantic Web: A new form of Web content that is meaningful
to computers will unleash a revolution of new possibilities." In
Linking the World's Information: Essays on Tim Berners-Lee's
Invention of the World Wide Web, pp. 91-103. 2023.

Ch. 16

Clarke, Roger. "Information technology and dataveillance."
Communications of the ACM 31, no. 5 (1988): 498-512.

Johnson, Steven. "Lou Montulli and the Invention of
Cookie: Hidden Heroes." Hidden Heros. Accessed August 28,
2024. https://hiddenheroes.netguru.com/lou-montulli.

Ch. 17

United Nations. "USE OF THE DARK WEB AND
SOCIAL MEDIA FOR DRUG SUPPLY." United Nations
Office on Drugs and Crime, 2023. https://www.unodc.org/
res/WDR-2023/WDR23_B3_CH7_darkweb.pdf.

YouTube video by Dr. Gareth Owen breaking down the
numbers on dark web services:
https://youtu.be/-oTEoLB-ses?si=b5VaHiTlLAnl3IZV

"Ross Ulbricht, the Creator and Owner of the Silk Road
Website, Found Guilty in Manhattan Federal Court on All
Counts." FBI, February 5, 2015. https://www.fbi.gov/contact-

us/field-offices/newyork/news/press-releases/ross-ulbricht-the-creator-and-owner-of-the-silk-road-website-found-guilty-in-manhattan-federal-court-on-all-counts.

"El Paquete Semanal: Alternativa Ante La Desconexión En Cuba." EL PAQUETE SEMANAL: ALTERNATIVA ANTE LA DESCONEXIÓN EN CUBA, 2024. https://paquetesemanal.eltoque.com/.

Ch. 18

Don't miss out!

Visit the website below and you can sign up to receive emails whenever Ryan Richardson Barrett publishes a new book. There's no charge and no obligation.

https://books2read.com/r/B-A-KJXCB-FPIWE

BOOKS 2 READ

Connecting independent readers to independent writers.

Did you love *The State of the Internet: Living on the Network of Networks*? Then you should read *Artificial Intelligence in Short*[1] by Ryan Richardson Barrett!

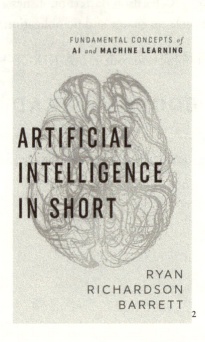

[2]

Artificial Intelligence in Short is a poignant book about the fundamental concepts of AI and machine learning. Written clearly and accompanied by numerous practical examples, this book enables any capable reader to understand concepts such as how computer vision and large language models are created and used while remaining free of mathematical formulas or other highly technical details. The tonality used in this book is unassuming and full of levity. The book maintains an even pace

---

1. https://books2read.com/u/merqlA

2. https://books2read.com/u/merqlA

that assists in conceptualizing the complex ideas of machine learning effectively while maintaining a clear but generalized focus in the narrative. Chapters develop through concrete concepts of computer science, mathematics, and machine learning before moving to more nuanced ideas in the realm of cybernetics and legislature. *Artificial Intelligence in Short* discusses the most up-to-date research in AI and computer science but also elaborates on how machines have come to learn and the historical origins of AI. The concepts of AI are outlined in relation to everyday life –just as AI has become a tool integrated into devices used daily by many people.

Read more at https://ryanrichardsonbarrett.com/.

Also by Ryan Richardson Barrett

Ossified Series
Ossified: A Story of Redemption

Standalone
Artificial Intelligence in Short
Artificial Intelligence in Short
Frick and Frack: A Comedy of Friends
The State of the Internet: Living on the Network of Networks

Watch for more at https://ryanrichardsonbarrett.com/.

About the Author

Ryan Richardson Barrett is a writer and cybersecurity professional from North Carolina who writes primarily about computer science and any subject that inspires him to learn and better himself.

Read more at https://ryanrichardsonbarrett.com/.